A HUNDRED HOURS TO SUEZ

An Account of Israel's Campaign in the Sinai Peninsula

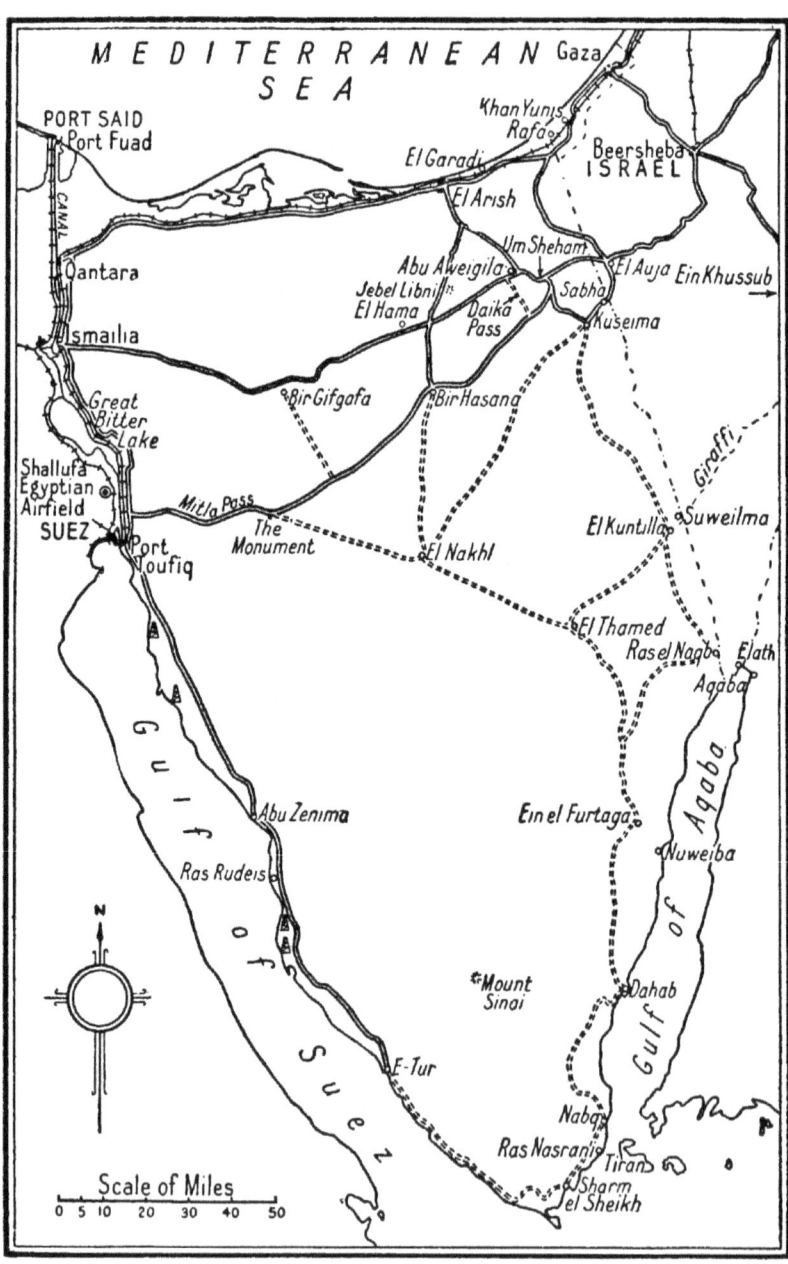

Robert Henriques

A HUNDRED HOURS TO SUEZ

An Account of Israel's Campaign in the Sinai Peninsula

19 57

NEW YORK : THE VIKING PRESS

COPYRIGHT © 1957 BY ROBERT HENRIQUES

PUBLISHED IN 1957
BY THE VIKING PRESS, INC.,
625 MADISON AVE., NEW YORK 22, N.Y.

Drawings by Yehuda Harari

AN UNCOMMON VALOR REPRINT EDITION
Printed in the United States of America

ISBN: 979-8869042125

Contents

Publisher's Note		ix
Author's Introduction		xi
I:	Sabras and This Book	3
II:	Israel Struck First	21
III:	The Spur of the Moment	29
IV:	The Plan	46
V:	An Airborne Brigade in the South	67
VI:	The Improbable Route	88
VII:	The Battles of the Center	107
VIII:	Victory in the North	129
IX:	Seen from the Air	152
X:	Sea View	165
XI:	What Prospects?	178

Publisher's Note

UPON reading the script of this book, received in New York by airmail on January 15, the publishers cabled their congratulations to Colonel Henriques and mentioned that there were two points which they thought American readers would like to see elaborated in the text. Could he give a more detailed accounting of the Russian supplies captured by the Israelis? Could he be more explicit about why Israel felt threatened when clearly so superior to Egypt militarily? Meanwhile the text was sent off to the printer to expedite production of the book.

Colonel Henriques, who was by that time in France, wrote back a few days later in answer to both of these points. Rather than delay the book by returning it to him in Europe to incorporate this material, we are quoting here from his letter:

"First, it is not possible to give a full account of Russian supplies captured, since the Israelis themselves never bothered to tot it up. This may seem strange—but then a lot of things are strange about Israel! I visited most of the dumps of captured equipment and saw enormous areas of ground covered by Russian tanks, antitank guns, troop carriers, etc. I could go where I liked and count what I liked—but nobody up to that time had done any official counting.

"As regards the second point, Israel felt (and definitely was) threatened by an Egyptian invasion. Although she defeated Egypt so decisively, she was far inferior to Egypt in military equipment and could not be at all sure that the Egyptian Army had not improved, with the help of Russian and German instructors and all this new equipment, during the eight years since the War of Independence. I have said this in Chapter IV. Nor was there any way of knowing how much more might be poured in to tip the balance with each week's delay.

"Moreover, it is quite possible that Egypt would not have been so easily defeated if she had been allowed to invade first, and the war had been fought on her own terms and at a time of her own choosing, and if the Unified Command of Arab States had made a concerted attack. Surprise is always a very important factor. Also, there were those 50 Russian bombers (Ilyushin 28), literally only minutes' flying time from Israeli cities, which never took the air against Israel. The reason was probably that the Egyptian air crews were not well enough trained to be operational, but their training would have been a great deal better in another few months' time."

Author's Introduction

THIS book was unpremeditated. Quite by chance I found myself in a position to write it and by the same chance decided to do so. The circumstances of that chance are described in the first chapter, which is in part a personal note and which might be an unwarrantable intrusion on a narrative, if it had any other purpose but to let the reader judge how far, and in what direction, the narrator is biased. It is something that I do not know myself. I know only that I have tried to tell the truth, so far as it was ascertainable, and that I was given every opportunity of ascertaining it.

Time was rather short. It was important that I should talk with military commanders, and visit with them the scenes of their battles, within a week or so after those battles, and before the edge had gone from their impressions. And it seemed important also that this account should be read as quickly as possible by as many people as possible. Therefore I was able to afford only seventeen days in which to meet everyone concerned and to travel about the Sinai Peninsula by car, jeep, and airplane, and another fourteen days in Tel Aviv in which to dictate what I had learned. On my return to England there was another week spent on pruning and rearranging the typescript, which had been censored in Israel. The censorship, as I have explained later, was very liberal and benevolent.

Following the precedent of T. E. Lawrence, I have not always been consistent over the spelling of names. Whereas his inconsistency was deliberate, mine is either accidental or due to ignorance. I cannot read either Hebrew or Arabic; and even if I could, the various maps of Sinai are all differently spelled; and anyway the Hebrew and Arabic alphabets tally neither with each other nor with our own. Moreover, the inconsistency and contradiction are characteristics of the Middle East. And although Israel is entirely a Western civilization, it is also entirely a part of the Middle East—two factors which, though they may seem to be a contradiction in themselves, will help to explain much that might otherwise be incomprehensible in the report that follows.

—ROBERT HENRIQUES

A HUNDRED HOURS

I

Sabras and This Book

THIS is an account of the 1956 Sinai Campaign, its origins, and its outcome. It is essentially a personal report, and I feel therefore that a brief explanation of the writer's attitude toward Israel, and of the circumstances in which this book was written, ought to be given at the start, so that the prejudice or objectivity—the validity—of what follows may be assessed.

I am a Jew who has always been a non-Zionist. I will not try to argue my case, except to say that our family has been established in England for two or three centuries—there is a genealogical dispute about which it is—and that we feel, or have felt, most of us, that we were Englishmen practicing the Jewish religion and yet, paradoxically, members of a people which had survived in its dispersion by reason of its faith, philosophy, and teaching. We had no answer to the racial perplexities; nor, as I see it, is any answer now visible in Israel herself. In England we may seem foreigners—perhaps from Spain whence we fled in the sixteenth century—but in Israel we would seem equally foreign alongside either the tough, usually blond, native Israeli, or the Oriental Jew from Syria, Iraq, Egypt, India, North Africa, Morocco, or the Yemen. Anyway, we felt ourselves assimilated in all but religion; and, to be honest, not many of us were particularly religious.

Because of this feeling, which had grown through a great many generations, we did not share the longing for Israel of the Jewish tradition. Moreover we doubted that that longing was really very widespread, except where it was promoted by the political Zionists. While we had always done what we could to succor the Jewish communities who were persecuted elsewhere, and to help large numbers of them to establish themselves in Britain, we did not believe that the solution to their problem—even after Hitler—was a Jewish state. We did nothing to hinder Zionism, but very little to help it.

The Zionist movement in Britain had not appealed to me for various reasons. Its political maneuvers in Anglo-Jewish affairs had not been above reproach. It had made rather a point of telling the established Anglo-Jewish families—whether of two generations or twelve—that they were of no account. Perhaps out of pettiness on my part, or perhaps for better reasons, I was inclined to accept the unkind definition of a Zionist as "a man who persuades a second man to give money to a third man to send a fourth man to live in Israel."

Moreover I had always resented the contention of so many Zionists that Anglo-Jewry needed Israel as a place of refuge against a possible outburst of anti-Semitism at home. All over the world, not least in Israel, I have argued with other Jews that "it can't happen here"—the "here" being Britain. They reply that the German Jews talked the same way before Hitler; they refer to anti-Semitic discrimination in the United States. I answer that the British people have peculiar qualities which make them quite different from either Germans or Americans; and that, even if anti-Semitism did become serious in my own country, I should not be disposed to leave it on that account. Indeed, a serious aggravation of anti-Semitism would be about the only factor that would keep me at home throughout an English winter. This kind of argument—the funk-hole argument—usually ended with a Zionist assurance that one day I should change my tune; one day I should need Israel, and Israel would receive me. And it is true today that Israel, by her Constitution, is compelled to give a home to any Jew who goes there and asks for citizenship.

Whatever my feelings toward the conception of Israel, they were overtaken by the creation of the state in May 1948. It now has a population of some 1,600,000 Jewish and some 130,000 Arab citizens. Yet even after its creation, and even after it had been subjected on its birthday to the coordinated attacks of five Arab Armies, and even after it had won its War of Independence, Israel was not much more than an item of news to me until the late autumn of 1955.

It was then that something clicked through some cause which, even today, I cannot locate. Perhaps it was the Centurion tank which Britain was giving to Egypt but withholding from Israel. Or perhaps it was some remote stirring in a Jew's blood. Whatever it was, I had a sudden, inexplicable, undefined and still indefinable feeling of identity with Israel, a place that I had never visited and for which I had even felt, hitherto, a kind of apprehensive repugnance.

By that time, after nearly thirty years of military service of one sort or another, I had been retired to the Reserve. I was a professional novelist and journalist, as well as a serious farmer. I wanted at least to pay a visit to Israel; but on what pretext could I do so? Doubtless I would be welcomed there as a tourist, the same as everyone else. But it was not as a tourist, I felt, that a Jew could go there. And even if I did, what would be my attitude on arrival? Curiosity? Appreciation which would scarcely fail to be privately patronizing? A sense that I had come as a Jew to claim my share of what had been done by others—that I was jumping on the bandwagon, so to speak? A sort of "sackcloth and ashes" repentance that I had never been a member of the band? A contrition which I could not honestly admit? Or would there be a chance, even at this late stage of achievement, of actually doing something to help? If only a Jew could go to Israel with the feeling, not that he needed Israel, but that Israel needed him, he would have a happier conscience.

In the spring of 1956 I wrote to the Israel ambassador in London giving him a synopsis of my life history and saying that if Israel were again engaged in war I would like to be able to do something about it. It was due to his generous reply that I first visited Israel in September and was allowed to meet some of the people who hold positions of responsibility there and a number of the senior officers of Israel's Army.

On the one occasion when I met Mr. David Ben-Gurion, it was at his home in Jerusalem. In an open-neck shirt he lay back in his chair, his hands clasped, his eyes half closed, talking for an hour about Israel, and the integration of her peoples ingathered from over sixty nations, and her need for peace. For much of the time he seemed to be thinking aloud; it was a most fascinating privilege to listen. For the past dozen years I had forgotten the impression that one gets from being in the company of one of the world's great men. It was a dozen years since I had gone to lunch at Chequers with Winston Churchill.

If you compare Winston Churchill at the age of seventy, a dozen years ago, with Ben-Gurion as he is today (he was seventy in October) the two men have quite a lot in common. Whereas Churchill's thoughts seemed to range around history, Ben-Gurion's seem to be traveling through the philosophies in their historical contexts. Both men are natural scholars, and their practical politics have always been related to their scholarship. Both are visionaries and, by comparison with ordinary men, seem to make up their minds with prophetic authority. Both have a keen sense of fun. Both have retained their youth long after it might have escaped them. Both are pugilists. Both are prone to a kind of naughtiness which is very endearing but can obviously be very troublesome. And both can descend with a bump to quite trivial personalities.

In the course of one such descent, Mr. Ben-Gurion inquired about myself. This gave me the opportunity to ask if I could possibly be of any use to Israel. He answered—yes, by bringing my younger children to visit Israel, to see the country for themselves before their lives became set. By then I had already realized that the elderly and the middle-aged could best help Israel through their offspring. But I persisted. "In the event of war?" I asked. Mr. Ben-Gurion admitted that, in the event of war, there might be occasions on which almost any active body might prove useful. I asked, "In that case what should I do?"

"Come, just come!" he said.

It was because of this reply that, having left Israel on October 3, I returned there on November 3 with a slight sense of grievance that the Israelis had finished their war before I could even get to it.

I also felt a fool. Nobody was unkind enough to tell me that I was useless; but when I revisited my old friends in their military offices, I found myself in the company of many others, all Israeli citizens of my own sort of age or younger, all ex-Army officers of my own rank or senior, all unemployed and unemployable. Some of them had been there for a week. Home seemed a shameful place when they were the youngest males in their neighborhood.

It is, of course, one of the occupational hazards of a military life that one very soon gets too old for it. This is particularly the case in the Army of Israel, where all the senior commanders in the field are in their middle thirties, and the chief of staff, General Dayan, at the age of forty-one, is about the oldest soldier employed in active operations. The Israel Army, by comparison with others, is one of extreme youth.

Youth was very gentle with us old people. It wanted to find us a job, but could think of nothing. It was a depressing day which seemed to take a month in passing.

In Israel nothing happens until it happens suddenly; nothing makes steady progress, but advances in a succession of leaps, pausing after each to consolidate. At midnight on Saturday I arrived. On Sunday I was unemployed, disguised as a free-lance journalist, with not even a newspaper at home to claim my allegiance. The next morning, Monday, I had breakfast in bed and started to read a paper edition of *Wuthering Heights*.

A friend walked into the bedroom, an Israeli Army officer. He sat on my bed and drank a cup of coffee while we discussed the remarkable misunderstanding of Israel which seemed to prevail throughout the world. Her public relations were shockingly inadequate. We drank orange juice while we agreed that the fault lay in

Israel's incompetence at this modern craft, and partly in her intense security and secrecy, which allowed her to disclose so little to the press, and to the diplomats, that nobody had a chance of knowing what her situation really was, of apprehending her needs, or understanding her actions. Nevertheless, it had to be admitted that this intense security maintained by every individual in the country, as well as officially, to an extent which far surpassed our own measures in Britain during our last war, was responsible for the complete surprise achieved at the start of the Sinai Campaign; and the surprise had been priceless in terms of lives saved, relatively bloodless victory, and time, precious time. On the other hand—

My friend interrupted our conversation to say, "Supposing you were to write a book about this campaign and its origins, and the situation which comes out of it; and supposing you could get that book published very quickly by your publishers in several different countries—"

I said that, with the security restrictions in force, nobody could even learn about these things, let alone write a book about them. But I sat up in bed when he answered, "In certain circumstances the security might, to some extent, be relaxed."

I asked, "Would there be a lot of strings attached to a book of this sort?"

"None at all," he said, "if they enabled you to write it." And there never was, at any stage of the process of producing this book, any attempt to influence my views, conclusions, criticisms, or phraseology.

An hour later I was discussing the project with a senior official in the Foreign Office. The same afternoon, Monday, I discussed it with that warm and remarkable woman, Mrs. Golda Meir, the foreign minister. On Wednesday I heard unofficially that the suggestion of this book had been approved in principle, subject to the Army's agreement. I heard nothing more on Thursday, Friday, Saturday morning. By noon it seemed clear that nothing would happen; that, anyway, the chance had been lost; the book should have been half-written already; it ought to be finished in a month. Once more I began to feel a fool, unwanted, useless. While I was making inquiries about an airplane home, the telephone rang. "It's okay," my friend said.

"What do you mean—okay?"

"It just is okay. You'll hear in due course."

"What do you mean—in due course?" But he had rung off.

The telephone rang again. This time it was a more senior Army officer. "It's okay," he said. This happened once more, before I went down to the bar to drink myself to sleep. The bar of the Dan Hotel was a grotesque place. The best part of two hundred correspondents were permanently established there, and all the languages of the world, with the exception of Hebrew, could be heard being cross. Although I had never been more than a dilettante journalist, I had met a dozen acquaintances, many of them ex-soldiers of several different nationalities, when first I entered the place. By now I knew scores, all of whom were united in a common fury against the public-relations set-up, and all consumed with rumor thriving in this newsless place. They imbibed rumor and liquor, nobody went to bed before midnight, and the bar was invariably crowded until three o'clock in the morning, sometimes until sunrise.

I slept for a few hours before I was summoned by telephone to a military office. Here I met an officer, an instructor at the Israel Staff College, which had dispersed when mobilization was ordered. Its teachers and students had been sent into the field on various useful jobs. The officer whom I now met, whose first name is Danny, had suffered, only a month previously, the tedium of hearing me lecture at the Staff College on what had once been my particular subject—planning.

Danny, a lieutenant colonel, had just got back from Sinai. Now he was to return there, taking me with him, introducing me to the various commanders and their staffs, escorting me by car, jeep, or plane to the sites of battles in the company of those who had actually taken part in them. He was to take me to the heads of all the departments in the War Office and to those of their staffs who could give me the information needed to write my book. He was also to acquire for me such maps, documents, translations, kits, equipment, and clothing as might be necessary. "I'm afraid this is an awful nuisance for you," I said to him.

"It's an order," he said agreeably. "I've been given it as a job." Although he was a Sabra—an Israeli born in Israel—he spoke excellent English, which he had learned while graduating in a British OCTU and serving as a British officer. I was to find that very few senior officers were unable to talk to me in my own language. They were nearly all Sabras.

"Sabra" is the name chosen for themselves by Israelis born in what is now Israel. Sabra is the fruit of the cactus. In order to eat it, you have to be an expert at cutting off those painful prickles and opening the shell to get at the edible heart. When you have done so, it is an acquired taste.

I cannot yet claim to have acquired that taste. The young Sabra —he matures into a much more pleasant character—is apt to seem brusque, even churlish. Except with a pretty girl, he is not very sociable toward strangers. He minds his own business and expects you to mind yours. Your business becomes his only when you need help and ask for it. To find the Sabra at his best you want to be in some kind of trouble, preferably in a dangerous area and preferably after dark, in the neighborhood of a *kibbutz* (a collective settlement). You will then be treated to boundless hospitality as a matter of course and helped with extreme competence. Otherwise you will be ignored. You will not be lifted up if you stumble in the street—nor will you be laughed at—and you will not get a smile of greeting when you exchange *shaloms* unless there is something particular to smile about. The Sabra will not usually thank you for giving him a lift in your car, but he is likely to shout at you crossly if you do not. The Sabra will rarely be punctual; he is always aggressively tough.

He is also aggressively equal. This is something which is passionately important to him, because equality and integration are, in Israel's context, synonymous. Israel is essentially a fragment of Western civilization in the middle of the Middle East, yet over half her population are of Oriental stock. In the process of integration the European or Russian Jew loses very little of his Occidental habits or characteristics, yet the Oriental Jew does not become westernized; in one or two generations both become Israelis—Sabras. Their origins are by no means forgotten but are unimportant. There is no "color prejudice"; and an Israeli of European origin has genuinely no distaste, not even in his deep subconsciousness, at the prospect of his sister's or daughter's marrying a dark-skinned or black Israeli of Oriental blood. The progeny of such a union will be not "half-caste" but Sabra. And the young Sabras will all be jumbled up together at school and, above all, in the Army during their national service.

This is what Israel means by "integration." Integration—the production of Sabras who will be fused into a nation with no social or economic distinctions—is one of her two great ideals. The other is peace. Peace is essential for the progress of integration. It is paradoxical that, up to the present, war and danger have been the most powerful integrating influences, and the Army the main integrating agent.

Most armies are organized in peace against the contingency of war. Israel's Army grew out of war and was afterward organized in peace. It was born as a fighting spirit, a determination to survive at the moment of her birth in 1948, and it grew up as a fighting experience which was always tempered, as Israel says, by her secret weapon: the fact that she had no alternative to victory; that defeat meant, not just the usual submission to the will of a conqueror, occupation by enemy troops, and all the other penalties that used to be paid by the vanquished, but quite simply extermination. It was only when the threat of extermination was annulled by the defeat of all five Arab Armies in 1949 that Israel's own Army, command, and staff could be properly organized. The organization that was then imposed upon the fighting spirit and experience of

Israeli soldiers was mainly of the British pattern. The spirit itself is typically and exclusively Sabra.

It is a strange spirit and not very easy to comprehend. Although Israeli units can be extremely smart on a ceremonial parade, there is very little discipline in the normal sense. Officers are often called by their first names amongst their men, as amongst their colleagues; there is very little saluting; there are a lot of unshaven chins; there are no outward signs of respect for superiors; there is no word in Hebrew for "sir." A soldier genuinely feels himself to be the equal of his officer—indeed of any officer—yet in battle he accepts military authority without question. I cannot explain, I cannot begin to understand, how or why it works. All my own military experience in the British and American Armies has taught me that first-class discipline in battle depends on good discipline in barracks. Israel's Army seems to refute that lesson.

This is all the more surprising because half the men of the Israel Army—following of course the general pattern of the country—are of Oriental stock. When Israel is engaged in battle with any of her neighbors, half the Israeli soldiers are of blood similar to that of the men on the other side and indistinguishable from them in appearance. What, then, is the process that turns the Oriental Israeli into a far better soldier than his counterpart in any of the Arab Armies, and what is the strange integrating agent that welds him, together with the Israeli of Occidental origin, into such a remarkable fighting force?

I asked General Moshe Dayan this question. He answered that, without doubt, the main integrating agent in the Israel Army was the Bible. This is difficult to understand, because Israel is not a very religious country, despite the considerable influence in civil affairs of the rabbinical courts. Yet I believe that Dayan's assertion is true. The Bible is Israel's history book; it is her source of wisdom from which an Israeli habitually quotes, and to which he refers when seeking a precedent, or a comparison, a metaphor, or a simile. It is much more than this, although I am quite unable to define it. Perhaps it is a religion in itself? I am unable to say, but I do know that very few Israelis would deny God, and that most of them have an unexpressed, or perhaps inexpressible, belief in divine inspiration—although relatively few of them practice any kind of religious observance.

The fact remains that Israel's Army is the result of some very remarkable integrating force. Dayan says that this force is the Bible. Dayan is as likely to be right as anybody else.

Moshe Dayan is a Sabra. He is the chief of staff of Israel's forces and the only serving officer who holds the rank of general. With his black patch over one eye and his electric personality, he is a remarkable leader of men and a military commander of genius or near-genius. He is forty-one years old.

Dayan's grandfather had been a scholar and writer in the Ukraine, and his father is now a member of the Knesset, which is Israel's Parliament. Moshe Dayan himself was born in Degania, a kibbutz which his parents had helped to establish as pioneers in what was then a desolate area encircled by swamps and looted periodically by Bedouin. When Moshe was six years old, his family moved to Nahalal, where they became founder members of the first cooperative settlement. Nahalal lies beneath the Galilee hills on good farming land, which perhaps persuaded Moshe's parents that their son should be a farmer. After he had finished his elementary education, he was sent to the agricultural school in Nahalal, which, incidentally, happens to be for girls. Moshe was the only male pupil.

Moshe himself wanted to be a farmer, but by 1929, when he was about twelve, the Arab attacks had become a perpetual menace and, like others of his age, he was enrolled as an armed night-watchman. In due course he became a member of Haganah, the Jewish defense force in Palestine. In 1935 he married Ruth Schwartz, a Jerusalem girl, and they went to England for their honeymoon. On their return they joined a settlement. But during the next year, 1936, the Arab revolts became such a menace to the British mandatory power that it organized a supernumerary police force in which Dayan was an instructor. The next year, 1937, he became a member of Orde Wingate's "Special Night Squad" and, later, Wingate's deputy.

In 1939, after the Round Table Conference, which is mentioned in Chapter XI, the mandatory power attempted to disband Haganah and arrested its leaders. Forty-two of them, including Dayan, were sentenced to ten years' imprisonment at one of the most farcical trials that have ever been staged under British jurisdiction. The sentence was commuted to five years, only two of which were actually served, because by 1941 the British had need of people like Dayan and pulled them out of jail to put them back into Haganah, which was once more recognized, for the moment, as an official organization.

In a Haganah unit serving on the Syrian border, Dayan got command of a reconnaissance detachment which was charged with helping the Australians in their advance into Syria, a country held at the time by Vichy France. In the course of operations deep behind the enemy lines, Dayan was wounded and lost an eye.

During the War of Independence, Moshe Dayan commanded a battalion on the Syrian front and made a dramatic return to his birthplace, Degania, as a victorious commander. Later he took Lydda with a handful of commandos against enormous odds. When the war was over, he returned to Britain and attended the Senior Officers' School alongside pupils from Egypt and other Arab countries. Back in Israel he held a number of Army appointments with competence and distinction, but without really revealing his remarkable gifts of leadership and military wisdom, which were scarcely suspected until he became chief of staff and was able to inspire the Israeli forces with his own imaginative interpretations of military doctrine.

The doctrine itself is not unorthodox. The training of Israel's Army is on normal lines, not very different from that of the British Army, except that it is much more rigorous and very, very good. I spent some time with the commander of the officers' school, studying the syllabus, measuring on the map the various exercises undertaken by the pupils and calculating the time-distance factors of various cross-country maneuvers. These were about fifty per cent tougher than the training standards of British Commando troops and American Rangers during the last World War.

Dayan demands "high standards of accomplishment" from all officers; but these standards are realistic, and he is severe on any senior commander who demands the impossible from his subordinates, yet still more severe on anyone who covers up a subordinate's mistake. Although anything that seems like a military error is ruthlessly investigated, Dayan's ultimate judgment is intensely human. Yet he will not admit that "failure to accomplish a mission" is excusable unless a unit has taken fifty per cent casualties. (Strangely enough, it was this doctrine that was responsible for the relatively minute *total* casualties of the Sinai Campaign.)

Dayan's insistence that the proper command for any officer is not "Go and do so-and-so" but always "Follow me!" is qualified. "A company commander should be with his forward platoon, but behind his leading section; a battalion commander should go with his forward company, but behind his leading platoons; a brigade commander should be with his leading battalion, but behind his forward companies." Dayan himself is apt to appear in the middle of a battle riding in a half-track alongside the leading battalion commander. "It was extremely disconcerting," a senior officer told me, "when Dayan's jeep came roaring up, just as we were going into El Arish and were being shot at by a few seventeen-pounders and a lot else. Still more disconcerting when he climbed into my half-track. When we cracked the position, he jumped off and started digging in the sand with his hands like a dog. He had seen some bits of Philistine pottery and was digging them up." Dayan is a very keen archaeologist.

"The commanding officer," Dayan says, "is not the most valuable man in the unit who must be insured against becoming a casualty. The most precious thing of any unit is the enemy objective that has to be captured." Remarks such as these suffer from translation. If he himself were saying them in English, they would have the same euphony of his speech in Hebrew. In either language he talks quietly, with a thoughtful, almost intent deliberation and with a phraseology that is precise and graceful.

Relaxed in his home, Dayan is a man of extreme simplicity and wide interests. On almost any subject he seems to be well informed and converses seriously but never without humor. His warmth on these occasions, and when he is amongst his men, contrasts strangely with the cold efficiency of his office. Sitting behind his desk in General Headquarters, he has no time at all for pleasantries or casual conversation. When any of his senior staff officers come to his office, it is for strictly practical purposes. In the discussions that follow he is liable to be vehement and even overbearing, a characteristic which, naturally enough, leads him to respect only those who stand up to him.

Dayan is a general who thinks in political terms. He has a great reverence for the prime minister—"We are all pupils of B. G."—and in his several semi-political jobs, before he became chief of staff, he showed great perception and shrewdness. In human relations, as well as in war, he is an excellent tactician. His one serious weakness, which he shares with the prime minister, is his contempt for public relations. If you try to argue with either Ben-Gurion or Dayan that no country now—let alone Israel—can hope to be understood by the world if it takes no steps to inform the world of its circumstances and aspirations, both men will smile in the most friendly fashion and change the subject. In this respect, perhaps, Dayan is a general of the old-fashioned British pattern.

People often ask who could replace Dayan if, in one of his various escapades when he appears in the forefront of a battle, he were to become a casualty. I should have said that this was no problem. I met at least half a dozen senior commanders, all of them in their early or middle thirties, who had enough personality, military knowledge, and experience of war to command a corps in the British or American Army. Perhaps none of them displays, as yet, that indefinable touch of something which lifts a first-class military commander into a national figure. But then, this touch was not apparent in Dayan until he assumed authority over all Israel's forces.

It is part of Dayan's talent that although his commanders are inspired with his own ruthless vigor and doctrine, they remain extreme individualists, inquiring, argumentative, and critical. Their criticism is applied to themselves as well as to everyone else. In the stories of battles that follow, I have tried to sketch the characters of some of these men. They all have to appear under pseudonyms, since Israel's "order of battle"—which means the identification of its formations and units—is still secret. (In all armies, while the possibility of war remains, the identity of commanders, which would disclose the identity of their units, is secret information.) Each commander, in his own peculiar way, was a man of impressive personality.

There were the two commanders of armored brigades, "Benyameen," who smashed the Egyptian armor in the central sector, and "Izzhak," who turned the royal road to Qantara into a litter of Egyptian tanks and transport: the former a quick, lithe, and inexorable man, a Rommel-like character, a huntsman on the battlefield; and the latter a sleepy, slow-moving person whose speed and decision in battle seem quite incompatible with his unaggressive, even gentle personality in his private encounters. There was "Udah," the rugged and volcanic commander of the infantry brigade which took Rafa, a man who boasts that he comes of the humblest peasant stock and whose outbursts of ferocious energy are punctuated by intervals of complete relaxation and epicurean enjoyment. And there was "Menachem," the commander of a naval squadron who was born, like Udah, in the humblest circumstances and who, as a host in his cabin, was the exact counterpart of an officer of the Royal Navy.

These were some of the many commanders to whom Danny introduced me. Nearly all of them were Sabras. Quite a number of them had been arrested, searched, questioned, and sometimes imprisoned, like Dayan, by the British mandatory power. Many of them can relate, when pressed to do so, some quite unpleasant experiences at the hands of that sometimes ignoble force, the Palestine Police. But practically none of them has the least feeling of bitterness toward Britain, and all of them hold the British people in astonishing affection. So far as I can recall, every senior commander has either served in the British forces—the Jewish Brigade, or the Eighth Army, or the Commandos, the Royal Air Force, the Royal Navy, or the Merchant Navy—or else has attended military courses in Britain during the past few years. Often they have done both. This fact made the accounts of their battles all the more interesting to me. It was illuminating to discover what tactical athletics could be evolved from British military teaching—and with what spectacular success. Moreover, our common education in the British Army or in British military establishments gave us a common language and usually enabled us to avoid using Danny as an interpreter in those rare cases when an Israeli officer's English was a little rusty.

Danny himself was a boyish, blond, and ruddy person, aggressively fit, almost hearty—indeed "a hearty" in the jargon of British universities. Always genial and unruffled, he was quite impervious to the bad temper of an elderly Englishman missing his cup of tea at sunrise in the desert. He is quite old for Israel's Army—thirty-four, to be exact, and he looks much less. For the three weeks he was my constant companion and guide, an instructor of infinite forbearance with myself and unsparing criticism of the events that we were jointly investigating.

Hence this book got itself written in the space of five weeks. Our researches began on November 13 and ended on the last day of the month. The writing had to be done in the following fortnight.

Danny and I had long conversations with over forty officers, not one of whom let me even suspect what I never knew until I was leaving Israel with the finished manuscript—that each had been given written orders to receive me and answer my questions. Only three times, in the course of all those conversations, was it necessary for Danny to interject briefly in Hebrew a warning that we were trespassing into a prohibited subject. He had his own instructions regarding security; but to this day I do not know, and cannot puzzle out, what were the prohibitions.

As each chapter was written it was submitted to a senior officer for censorship. He has made remarkably few deletions and none at all for any reasons other than security. In no single case has he suggested that criticism should be modified. Only when I was hopelessly wrong on a point of fact has he suggested any amendment; and in such cases he has always insisted that whether or not I accept his suggestion was entirely my own concern. Twice I have been able to extract from him an admission that, in his view, I have drawn wrong conclusions from right facts. Otherwise, nobody has ever tried to impress opinions on me or indeed to do anything but disclose the facts as fully as possible and let me make up my own mind about them.

Nor have my feelings about the Egyptians been acquired in Israel. Indeed I have found that Israelis are tolerant of all their Arab neighbors, not excluding Egypt, and even have for them a kind of affection which I cannot share myself. The nomadic Arab is one thing—I have always felt—but the Egyptian quite another. Many years ago I wrote a book about the nomadic, cattle-owning Arabs of the Sudan. Like so many other Englishmen, I thought I understood them and I regarded them with an affection which is certainly not extinguished. My assessment of the Egyptian was first made at an even earlier date, nearly thirty years ago when, as a very junior subaltern, I was serving in the British Army in Egypt. Everything that I have since seen and learned of the Egyptian has confirmed my original judgment. In general, Israelis would not agree with me. They have different ways of thought and a forbearance, patience, and generosity greater than I shall ever possess.

This aspect of the Israeli character seems at variance with my impressions of the Sabra. But it is no good trying to explain discrepancies in any account of anything in Israel. Israel is full of contradictions; and it is not really very surprising that the brusque, churlish, and aggressively tough young Sabra should grow into a military commander with a distinguished personality and a courteous approach.

Anyway, it is no good my pretending to understand Israel's Army. I know quite a lot about its organization, equipment, training, and tactics. I have spent some time with it and have much enjoyed the experience. But understanding is another matter. The most that I can hope to do in this book is to describe what Israel's Army did and how and why, and to trust that the story will somehow or other provide its own explanation of what that Army is.

In a farewell conversation, Danny said, "I want you to know that the warmth and frankness of all the officers we visited was something quite exceptional in Israel. They are all busy men and normally they would have obeyed their orders to receive us but would have got rid of us as quickly as possible. Why didn't they? It was not politeness, and not because they liked us, but because they all believed in the importance of this job—as I do myself. . . . The Sabra," Danny said, "has in his blood a belief in the power of books."

II

Israel Struck First

ON THE afternoon of Thursday, October 25, 1956, Israel began to mobilize. At a Cabinet meeting on Sunday, October 28, Israel took the decision to launch an operation against Egypt, although the size and scope of that operation were not then determined. At nightfall on Monday, October 29, a battalion of an airborne brigade was dropped in the Mitla area, not far from the Suez Canal, and the rest of that brigade moved across the frontier to reinforce it. One hundred hours later Israel's Army, in response to the British ultimatum, halted just short of Suez.

The story of what happened after October 25 will not make sense without some account of what went before it and some explanation of why Israel took this action at the time she did. Yet to trace the historical origins of the Sinai Campaign is a long business which can to advantage be postponed until the end of this book, where I must try to view the campaign, not as an isolated incident, but in the context both of past events and of future prospects. That attempt is bound to be controversial and, since it must be supported by dates, quotations, and statistics, cannot be brief.

For the moment I shall do my best to be both brief and uncontroversial in recounting the events that caused Israel to take military action. I shall try to confine myself to facts which are indisputable. If anyone does dispute them, he can find in Chapter XI their statistical and historical proof.

By a resolution of the United Nations the State of Israel came into existence on May 14, 1948. On that day she was attacked by the Armies of Lebanon, Syria, Jordan, Iraq (operating through Jordan), and Egypt. Hostilities were concluded by a series of armistice agreements that were signed at various dates in 1949 with each of those Arab states, except Iraq. (Iraq is still technically at war with Israel.) The preamble to each of these armistice agreements stated that their purpose was "to facilitate the transition from the present truce to permanent peace in Palestine." During the seven years that followed, no peace treaties between Israel and any of the Arab states were negotiated. The Arab states refused to recognize Israel's existence. Egypt insisted again and again, and in categorical terms, that she considered herself to be still at war with Israel.

Throughout this period Egypt continued to make war against Israel by all the means at her disposal. Until recently she had no chance of successfully renewing her invasion of Israel. Hence, while her preparations for invasion were accelerated with Russian assistance, her warlike measures were confined to economic blockade and *fedayeen* raids against civilian objectives. Perhaps the most formidable of these measures was her blockade of all ships trading with Israel and passing through the Suez Canal. When this was brought to the UN in 1951, Egypt sought to justify her actions on the grounds that she was still at war with Israel. (The illegality of these measures under the 1888 Convention—war or no war— can be left out of the argument at this juncture.) On September 1, 1951, the Security Council, with Russia consenting, called upon Egypt to stop the blockade forthwith. The blockade has continued ever since.

Egypt next extended her blockade to the Gulf of Aqaba. To enter the gulf all shipping must pass through a narrow channel west of the island of Tiran. Opposite Tiran there were two small hamlets of Arab fishermen—Ras Nasrani and Sharm El Sheikh. These two places were evacuated of their inhabitants and very heavily fortified with naval batteries and a garrison of over two thousand men. All trade to and from Israel's port of Elath at the head of the gulf was completely stopped, a measure which could be justified only on the grounds that Egypt was at war with Israel.

To augment the blockade of Israel's shipping, the Arab League organized an economic boycott. It allowed no trade or communication of any sort between its members and Israel. Its members refused to trade with any firm that traded with Israel. (For instance, when the Ford Motor Company proposed to establish an automobile factory near Haifa, they were prevented from signing the contract by the threat that it would mean the banning of all their vehicles from all Arab countries.) The boycott was extended to operate not only against Israel but against all Jews of all nationalities, and any firm who wanted to tender for a contract with members of the Arab League was required to declare the number of its Jewish employees and Jewish directors and the degree of Jewish control and management.

The boycott spread into other fields. Most of the international agreements governing air traffic were abrogated by the Arab League. No aircraft which was bound to or from Israel might fly over Arab territory. No aircraft that had called at Lydda could land at the airport of any Arab state, no matter what the emergency. No communication between ground and air, such as meteorological warnings or flight directions, was permitted to aircraft of any line which had called at Lydda. The issue of flight information from Lydda was jammed.

The boycott then reached into the domestic circles of the UN itself. Members of the Arab League refused to send delegates to some of the regional meetings of the UN's specialized agencies, if Israel was sending delegates. No delegate from Israel was allowed to attend any conference of any of the specialized agencies held in any Arab state. Some of the Arab states refused to allow Jewish officials of the specialized agencies—no matter what their nationality—to attend conferences held in their countries.

None of these measures of boycott were reciprocated by Israel.

Most of them, of course, were not actually illegal, but only incompatible with any notion of peace. Only the blockades exercised both in Suez and in the Gulf of Aqaba depended for their actual legality on the assumption that a state of war existed. But the sum total of all these measures was having very grave consequences on Israel's economy.

Meanwhile there was active warfare on Israel's frontiers. The fedayeen raids had increased in intensity. They were directed exclusively against civilian targets and, although only a few men, women, and children might be killed or wounded in any one incident, the sum total had made it necessary to evacuate certain of the frontier settlements whose members were recent immigrants of Oriental stock and so were less seasoned to withstand the conditions of constant danger. The fedayeen were organized, trained, and paid by the Egyptian Army. Their main headquarters was at Khan Yunis in the Gaza Strip, but from 1955 they had been operating also from bases in Jordan and Syria. Some of these bases were in charge of Egyptian officers; others were under the control of the Egyptian military attachés.

Until the summer of 1955 Egypt denied responsibility for the fedayeen raids, but on August 26 she acknowledged them officially and acclaimed the fedayeen as national heroes.) Documents which were taken by Israel in the Gaza Strip disclose the full scope of the fedayeen organization, the rates of pay, the organization of training, and the operational directives. I have seen a photostat copy of a "Distinguished Conduct Certificate" issued from "General Headquarters of the Armed Forces, Gaza District," by Captain Galaat Suleman Galby to Sergeant Al Saud Hassan Dahasma, testifying that he "carried out completely his sacred mission on the soil of Palestine, on 28/5/56, within the Israeli borders, and showed an excellent example by his manly conduct, courage, and valor, acted with exemplary discipline, high morale, and gallantry, and he is a man who understands and appreciates discipline and worships it."

Israel's frontiers are quite indefensible against this kind of infiltration. Her only means of defense was what has become known as the "reprisal raid," a recognized military recourse which was employed, for instance, by the British in defense of the Northwest Frontier. These reprisal raids by Israel were always directed against military objectives and usually against bases or headquarters of fedayeen activities. For instance, the reprisals at Khan Yunis in the Gaza Strip, and on the police stations at Gharandal, Rahwa, and Kalkilya were all directed against fedayeen headquarters, known as such to Israel's Intelligence Service.

Meanwhile Egypt's military deployment in Sinai, and the massive bases which she had built up in the area of El Arish, could be intended only for forthcoming operations of a more orthodox military nature against Israel. It was a matter of speculation when these operations would actually be launched, and the date would depend on Egypt's relations with the rest of the world. She would have to settle the Suez problem before she could risk launching a full-scale campaign against Israel.

That this campaign was being prepared was proved conclusively by documents captured at Gaza. For instance, I have seen a photostat copy of a "most secret" training directive: "Directive No. 2 by Commander of the 6th Infantry Division" addressed to "Commander Egyptian area in Palestine and Commander of the Reinforced 5th Infantry Brigade." It is dated February 23, 1956. Paragraph I states: *"Introduction*—Every officer must prepare himself and his subordinates for the inevitable struggle with Israel with the object of realizing our noble aim—namely, the annihilation of Israel and her destruction in the shortest possible time and in the most brutal and cruel battles." Paragraphs 2 to 6 deal respectively with military training, commanders, weapons and equipment, fortifications, and visits that were to be paid by commanders of other formations in the Sinai Peninsula. Paragraph 7 lays down the state of readiness which the various brigades were to reach by April 1, 1956. Paragraph 8 concludes the document as follows:

"Our aim is always: the destruction of Israel. Remember and act to achieve it."

In pursuit of this aim Egypt had collected arms and military equipment from every possible source. From Britain she had got 41 Centurion tanks (9 in 1950 and 32 in 1955), 200 Archers, which are tank-destroyers consisting of seventeen-pounder guns mounted on a Valentine tank chassis (1955), 70 jet planes, Vampires and Meteors (1950), 150 guns of different calibers, 20 heavy bombers, Lancasters and Halifaxes, and a plant for the production of Vampires and Venoms, a license being given by the de Havilland factory (1952). The two Z class destroyers which were sold to Egypt in 1955 were matched by the same number sold to Israel at the same time.

The United States had sold Egypt two frigates of the *Colony* type in 1952 and 600 four-wheel-drive military vehicles in 1953. In 1954 and 1955 Italy sold Syria 30 Vampires which flew straight to Egypt.

In the meanwhile the other members of the Arab League were similarly arming themselves. In the case of Jordan and Iraq, arms were supplied by Britain under her treaties with those countries. Iraq, with whom Israel was still technically at war, had 42 Centurion tanks and 30 Vampires and Venoms, amongst much other equipment, from Britain; and from the United States, 30 armored cars of the M.8 Greyhound type. Jordan, from whose territory the fedayeen were operating, had purchased in 1955 a number of the newest British tank-destroyers, the "Charioteers," which are twenty-pounder guns on Cromwell chassis, and had received as a gift from H. M. Government 10 Vampires. That same year the Saudian Army, which got all its equipment from the United States, had been able to buy six Convair transport planes—although the sale of these planes was at that time prohibited in the United States—and in 1956 purchased 18 light tanks of the M.41 Walker-Bulldog type and 18 medium tanks, M.48. During the period between January 1951 and June 1956, Britain alone had sold, to the countries of the Arab League, military and para-military equipment, including civil aircraft, amounting to 27 million pounds sterling, whereas what she had sold to Israel amounted to 3.26 million pounds sterling. (Israel, incidentally, had not been allowed to purchase any heavy tanks to match the Stalin and the Centurion.) These deliveries of arms were of course nothing compared with those that had been received by Egypt under the Czecho-Egyptian Arms Purchase Treaty of October 1955, and were being received by Syria under a similar purchase treaty signed in 1956. Egypt had got, or was getting, 50 heavy tanks (Stalin III), 150 medium T.34 tanks (85-mm. gun), 200 armored troop carriers (BTR 152), 100 self-propelled guns (SU 100 tank-destroyers), 120 MIG 15 fighter aircraft, 50 twin-engined jet bombers (Ilyushin 28), 20 transport planes (Ilyushin 14), 2 destroyers of the *Skory* class, 15 fast mine-sweepers, 2 submarines, 200 anti-tank guns (57 mm.), 50 guns (122 mm.), 100 five-ton vehicles (Zis 150), 50 ten-ton vehicles (Praga), 400 scout cars (GAS), a consignment of radar anti-aircraft with 85-mm. guns, a thousand recoilless rifles (firing a bomb of 82 mm.) and many thousands of semi-automatic Czech and Russian rifles and Bakelite mines. The Syrians, under their treaty, were receiving 100 medium tanks (T.34), 100 MIG 15 fighters, numbers of armored troop carriers, anti-aircraft guns with radar, 122-mm. howitzers, 122-mm. guns, 152-mm. howitzers, and large quantities of semi-automatic Czech rifles.

With the Russian equipment, of course, there had come to Egypt numerous Russian technicians and instructors to augment the German instructors who had been at work on the Egyptian Army for some years past. With the Russian instructors there had come numerous other "advisers" and "experts."

Again and again throughout the years following the armistice agreements of 1949, Israel had appealed for peace both to the countries of the Arab League, individually and jointly, and to the UN. She had appealed to the UN against the acts of war which Egypt had been conducting. The UN had been able to do nothing at all about it. Although a resolution of the Security Council amounts to an international order—whereas the General Assembly can issue only recommendations—no steps whatever had been taken to implement the Security Council resolution of September 1, 1951, calling upon Egypt to desist from her illegal blockade. It was abundantly clear to Israel that she could count on no help from the UN. At that time it seemed equally clear that she could depend for help on no sources other than her own.

In October 1956 it was proposed that Iraqi forces should enter Jordan to reinforce her internal security. Iraq was still technically at war with Israel. One of the terms of Israel's armistice agreement with Jordan had been that Iraqi forces must withdraw from the latter's territory. The threat of their return seemed to constitute a warlike act on the part of both Jordan and Iraq. It was then that Britain issued a solemn warning to Israel that, if she responded with warlike measures against Jordan, Britain would be bound to take military action against Israel under the Anglo-Jordan Treaty.

Then came the Jordan elections, which produced a pro-Egyptian majority. Egypt began immediately to send military aircraft, tanks, and other heavy equipment to Jordan, and followed this with a visit of her chief of staff, General Amer. On October 24 the Unified Command of Arab States under General Amer was established, thus putting a military seal on the encirclement of Israel. The next day Israel began to mobilize.

It adds up to this. Egypt insisted that she was still at war with Israel. She had waged that war in the modern sense with every means at her disposal, except invasion by organized military forces. She had not yet resorted to invasion because she was otherwise occupied with the Suez Canal crisis and because her prospects of success against Israel were not yet sure. Those prospects were improving daily and had been substantially advanced by the receipt of warlike equipment from Russia, and now by the establishment of the Unified Command of Arab States under Egypt's chief of staff. It was only a matter of time—and a short time at that—before Egypt would strike. Israel struck first.

III

The Spur of the Moment

THIS chapter tells the story of the four days—the first period of a hundred hours—between the evening of Thursday, October 25, when mobilization was ordered, and the evening of Monday, October 29, when operations began in Sinai.

It is obvious that many people are interested in this period from the point of view of whether or not there was "collusion" among the British, French, and Israeli governments. A few whispered words between three statesmen would, I suppose, have constituted "collusion." Personally I am convinced that the whispering did not in fact take place. But I cannot prove it.

On the other hand, there is an enormous weight of evidence to suggest that, if Israel had any idea in advance of the action that Britain and France were to take, it was only in vague terms; that it was nothing more than a conclusion drawn—without the need for much perspicacity—from an acquaintanceship with international affairs; that it was uncertain knowledge and highly undependable, and that it did not in any way influence Israel's initial action. Undoubtedly it had a substantial effect on the progress of the campaign. It prevented Israel from establishing herself on the Suez Canal and thus opening the canal for her own shipping as well as for the shipping of everybody else. It saved (as will be shown) about one-third of the Egyptian Army from destruction or disintegration. And it probably saved Nasser.

Those are my own conclusions about the probability of "collusion" and about the effects of Anglo-French intervention on the Sinai Campaign. On the former subject, the evidence can only be circumstantial; but it mounts up to quite a weight and it will be found scattered throughout the chapters of this book, though a great deal of it is in the pages that follow immediately. On the latter subject, the evidence is conclusive that Israel would be in a better position now if the British and French had kept out of the active operations.

It may seem strange, but it is an undoubted fact that Israel's mobilization came as an enormous relief to her people. For the previous six or seven years there had been no peace anywhere near her frontiers—and no part of Israel is very far from her frontiers—and for the past two years there had been the continuous attacks by fedayeen on civilian targets. The economic war of the blockade in the Gulfs of Suez and Aqaba, and with it the boycott, had done great harm to Israel's economy and caused much hardship to her people. The knowledge that Egypt and other countries of the Arab League were amassing vast quantities of arms, and that the Egyptian Army was deployed in the Gaza Strip and in the Sinai Peninsula preparing for invasion, created, as it was intended to do, an atmosphere of disquiet and suspense. It is worth remembering that, technically and in fact, the state of Israel has never been at peace during the whole of her life.

When mobilization was ordered that evening, everything changed overnight. Instantly the intolerable strain was broken. At last there was something active being done which put an end to the tension of passive endurance. I was not in Israel at the time and I failed to get there (as I have told) until the hundred hours of mobilization plus the hundred hours of the campaign were past. But it is unanimously reported that Israel accepted mobilization neither with apprehension nor with enthusiasm, but with feelings of plain, simple relief.

It was remarkable how little the country was dislocated by the call-up of so many young and middle-aged men and women. "Sorry if the service is slow," apologized the maître d'hôtel of Herzliya's fashionable Accadia, on Friday, October 26, as tourists crowded the dining room for lunch, "but half an hour ago three waiters were mobilized, and I am left with only one piccolo."

"I am so sorry, madam," said the receptionist of another hotel, "but the manager was called away suddenly. When will he be back, madam? Maybe a few hours, maybe a few days, maybe a week or two."

On the next day, Saturday, October 27, there was "business as usual" in the diplomatic corps and a UN cocktail party was held. At this function the diplomats were agreed that, in view of the expectation that Iraqi troops would be entering Jordan within a matter of hours, Israel was clearly and reasonably preparing for action on the Jordan frontier. An ambassador, leaving the cocktail party in evening dress on his way to an official dinner, was driving his own car. His chauffeur had been mobilized that morning. Another diplomat complained of a sore finger; he had spent the whole day typing a letter, since his secretary had been called up.

"Security" seemed to be very lax at last. You could learn—"on the best possible authority, but for God's sake don't say that I told you"—that 200,000 Iraqi troops were massed in Jordan, that the whole Israel Army was waiting to meet them, and that the U.S. Sixth Fleet had come to Israel's aid and was already at Haifa.

By the next day—Monday—faces were grave. Mobilization had been ordered nearly four days previously, and nothing had yet happened. The situation must be disastrous. French paratroops were waiting at Cyprus; and war between an alliance of France and Israel on the one hand and an alliance of Britain and the Arab League on the other had already started. American "refugees" were being evacuated.

On Tuesday the news broke that there had been some kind of operation, not against Jordan at all, but on the Egyptian frontier. Relief was restored to the population. The blackout was ordered, so that there were long queues of people trying to buy black paper. When it ran out, they bought red paper. When that ran out, they bought anything else that might seem to comply with the regulations. If anybody had a long-term plan to start hostilities at this moment, it was strange that he had taken no steps to provide Israel's population with the means of taking the most elementary air-raid precautions. Egypt had 50 of the Ilyushin 28s, the latest thing in Russian medium bombers. The first casualties of the campaign were those of old gentlemen—"Hand me the hammer, love!" —who fell off chairs while trying to contrive a blackout.

The traditional kind of jokes, with which we have been made familiar throughout the world by Jewish comedians, were of course irrepressible. A young woman who keeps a flower shop in Tel Aviv put up a notice: "Shop closed. Gone to meet Nuri. Back in a week." It was truer than she thought. Another woman told her friends, "On Friday I parted from my son; on Sunday from my daughter; on Monday from my husband. And now what do they do but take my motor car." A soldier who found himself with his unit on the eve of his wedding day was consoled by his comrades: "Don't let it worry you! Your bride was mobilized too; so was the rabbi; and the guests won't turn up, because they are also in the Army."

As the operations continued into the second and third days, there was very little news of what was happening. Indeed most of the news came from the Egyptian and Jordan broadcasting stations, which were reporting great victories for Egypt, thousands of Israelis killed and many thousands more taken prisoner, and stupendous booty. Of course nobody believed it. There was no run on the banks. Nobody was hoarding food; the shops in Israel's cities were no more crowded than usual: it was the end of the month, and nobody had any money.

In any country there are different scales of mobilization, and it is carried out by stages. Certain classes are called up in the first instance, and others a few days later, others later still—and so on. I do not know the scale on which Israel mobilized, but it was obviously large. It has always been well known that, with total mobilization, Israel could put some quarter of a million men and women into her armed forces. The vast majority of these would be called up into their reserve units.

Israel's economy cannot support anything more than the minimum standing Army. This consists of its senior officers and a few key personnel. There are not more than "several" regular brigades which are composed of national service men on a framework of regular officers and senior NCOs. Their task is threefold: to maintain the minimum force necessary for local defense; to train men who have been called up for national service; and to provide a "school" for the reserve brigades.

The size of the standing Army varies from time to time, since the size of the "call-up" varies, not only according to the number of boys and girls reaching the age of eighteen in any year, but also according to the number of immigrants. And the size of the forces available at any moment can be adjusted by the recall for annual training of reserve officers and men to their reserve brigades and units. It happened that, at the moment when the Sinai Campaign was ordered, the forces available were at their minimum strength. The annual training of reserves had been completed during the previous spring and summer, and the officers and men had been dispersed, some time previously, to their civilian occupations.

This question of the size of forces under arms at the end of October is significant. If, for instance, a few reserve brigades had been called up for training on, say, October 20, the size of the forces immediately available would have been increased by a very substantial proportion. And if the operations had been planned in advance, the obvious recourse would have been to call up a few brigades for training at the appropriate moment. In fact, not one single reserve brigade that was employed in the campaign was under training at the time when mobilization was ordered. The NCOs and men of these reserve brigades, as well as most of the officers, were farming, building, plumbing, painting and decorat-

Boys and girls both do national service

ing, clerking, shop-keeping, or working on the factory bench when they got the message that they were to report to a prearranged destination.

A reserve brigade is a local or regional affair whose members all live in the same district. Its commander and his senior staff are regular officers. Everybody else, except for perhaps one clerk at the headquarters of each unit, is on the reserve and is employed full-time on his or her civilian occupation. Women on the reserve are trained exactly the same as men, except that those who have children are excused from national service—always provided that they have remembered to register and confirm their claims to parenthood at the appropriate headquarters. A reserve unit corresponds exactly to a unit of the Territorial Army in Britain, or (I believe) to a National Guard unit in America. Its officers and men are required to report for training for a day a month, or for a period of three consecutive days every three months, at the commander's discretion. In addition, they have a period of annual training of several weeks, which cannot by law exceed a month, and which corresponds to the "annual camp" of a British territorial unit.

It will be seen that the men of the reserve brigades get no more training than the men of the British Territorial Army. On the other hand, they have been more intensively trained—I should say better trained—during their period of national service, which is two and a half years for men and two years for women. But I doubt if the British Territorials or the U.S. National Guard could hope to meet the demands that war made on Israel's reserves. It was asking a great deal of civilians to take them from their homes, and often their sedentary occupations, and put them into battle in reserve *infantry* brigades not more than four or five days later. But it was done successfully. And it is asking much, much more of a reserve *armored* brigade, whose organization and equipment demand, nowadays, very high standards of training and technical competence, to commit it to a severe and protracted engagement within six days of mobilization. This was done also. Indeed the reserve brigades, both infantry and armored, not only have gone into battle, but have come out of it victorious, within eight days of the issuing of the first mobilization orders.

There are two methods of mobilization in Israel: silent mobilization and mobilization by radio. The radio method entails broadcasting a series of code names—each representing a particular group or unit—followed by an announcement of the time when these men and women are required to report at a prearranged rendezvous. The orders for all such radio transmissions have to be signed by the prime minister. On one occasion, Mr. Ben-Gurion objected strongly to writing his name immediately beneath the words "Sleeping Beauty." But this was the code name for a group that was to be mobilized for training.

It was the "silent" method that was used for mobilization before the Sinai Campaign. This method takes place in four phases and begins with a message to the regular officer or NCO in each reserve unit. As soon as he gets his orders, he calls up a small, preselected group of men who drive round the area issuing orders to the rest of the personnel and giving them twenty-four hours in which to report to their mobilization centers. Provided the receipt of any order has been signed by a member of the man's (or woman's) family over the age of eighteen, it is legally assumed to have been received and to be operative. This is the second phase of mobilization.

The third phase consists of "marrying" the reservists to their mobilization stores. This is something which can be practiced in advance. But the fourth phase, which consists of providing each unit with requisitional civilian transport, cannot be made a drill. It entails the most complicated kind of prearrangement and—as will be seen in the narratives that follow—takes considerable time and is very vulnerable to dislocation.

The vehicles trickle in, after their orders reach them, accompanied by their civilian drivers. If a driver—no matter what his age—says that he wants to go to war along with his vehicle, he is allowed to do so. After all, it is his property, and sometimes his only property; and he knows best how to coax it into mobility or to persuade it to negotiate the thick sand or punitive rocks of a tricky passage. In Israel the older civilian drivers compose an elite section of society. Most of them took part in the War of Independence; they know the country in intimate detail; they are tough individuals who make it a matter of pride to keep their vehicles moving, no matter what the terrain, and they are accepted as honored comrades when they choose to become part of the unit to which their vehicles have been allotted.

Once the vehicles, and maybe their drivers with them, have reported to a unit or brigade, that unit or brigade is ready to move. It then gets orders to drive to its assembly area. At some stage of this drive it passes out of the command which has been responsible for its mobilization and enters the new command—Southern Command in the case of the Sinai Campaign—which is to be responsible for its operations. Southern Command then had to take charge of its movements, to feed it and supply it, and to send it to an assembly area where it would be concentrated within its appropriate task force. To this assembly of brigades and units the task-force headquarters was then added; and when it arrived, it took over command and became an operative military formation. Mobilization was then completed.

On Saturday, October 27, the first military units to mobilize had started moving south to their assembly areas in the Negev. By Sunday, the frontier *kibbutzim* all over Israel—from those facing Lebanon, Syria, and Jordan in the north and east, to those facing Egypt in the south and southwest—were in a state of readiness and of permanent defense. Anybody who visited any of the kibbutzim along the Sinai border and along the Gaza Strip during that weekend, or who tried to get south along the road to Beersheba, must have been aware that very substantial movements of troops and other warlike preparations were taking place. These could have been interpreted as precautionary measures that would naturally have to be taken, in view of the existence of the Unified Command of Arab States, if hostilities with Jordan were imminent. But the scale of these movements was such that no military observer could escape the conclusion that operations, whether defensive or offensive, were at least being contemplated in the southern area. Presumably this information would be sent to their respective war departments by the various military attachés.

At the same time, the mere fact of mobilization was no proof, and only dubitable evidence, that a campaign was actually imminent. In the past there had frequently been partial mobilizations, sometimes for training purposes and sometimes when a large-scale reprisal was to be undertaken against fedayeen bases. In the latter case the Army often called up more men than it needed, as an insurance against the operations' developing or expanding or exploding beyond the scope that was intended. And although the mobilization of October 25 was on a larger scale than ever before, it might have been a preliminary to nothing more than a particularly large-scale reprisal, or it might have been a bluff. It is interesting and appropriate to speculate what happened in the various war departments (or war offices) abroad during that weekend, or on the Monday morning, when the messages that were presumably sent by the military attachés in Israel began to arrive.

Every army has a planning section which works on the highest level, preparing plans for any contingency. It is inconceivable that the British, French and the United States would not have prepared plans in detail for such events as war between Israel and Jordan, offensive operations by Egypt against Israel, and offensive operations by Israel against Egypt. It is also inconceivable that the foreign military attachés in Israel were not, by this time, warning their governments of the probability of operations in the south. After receiving such warnings it would be normal for the planning section in each country to unlock the appropriate filing cabinet and produce, for the use of the chief of staff and cabinet, the plans dealing with this contingency. I have no means of knowing what happened, but my guess is that events in Washington, London, and Paris took that course. My guess goes further. It would surprise me if the general staffs in London and Paris had not made plans to take advantage of a situation in which Egypt was involved with Israel.

During that same weekend in Israel it seems that neither the government nor General Headquarters was unduly disturbed. On the Friday, the day after mobilization began, Mr. Ben-Gurion wrote me a gracious letter in reply to the usual "courtesy note" which, on my return from my first visit to Israel, I had sent him from England. Since the Israel postal services do not operate on a Saturday, the Sabbath, this letter was postmarked in Jerusalem on Sunday, October 28. It got to my home in Gloucestershire on the same day that my airplane landed in the blackout at Lydda airport.

On Saturday, October 27, General Dayan gave his final orders in preparations for the Sinai Campaign. The orders were to take effect if the government decided on the following day that the first military moves against Egypt—the dropping of a parachute battalion at Mitla—were to be made. Dayan then returned to his home near Tel Aviv and spent a long evening piecing together fragments of a Byzantine vase which he had recently dug up. This is his favorite relaxation.

That same Saturday evening, the prime minister came down with flu. He had a temperature of 39.9 degrees centigrade, which is over 103 degrees Fahrenheit. So far as I remember, this was the day when, according to some reports, he was supposed to be in Paris engaging in "collusion" with the French government. In fact, Mr. Ben-Gurion was in Israel throughout the whole of September and October; and every day can be accounted for in detail by his secretarial staff, if anybody thinks it worth while to inquire. Between October 27 and October 30, Mr. Ben-Gurion was keeping himself operational by the use of "Palgin" tablets.

Despite his illness, Mr. Ben-Gurion, seventy years old, paid a visit to the president on Sunday, October 28. That night the prime minister's home presented a battlefield between the heads of political factions in the Knesset and the doctors, the latter losing the engagement; meanwhile, in Washington, President Eisenhower sent for the ambassadors of Britain and France. The news of this meeting, and the possible implication that the United States, Britain, and France might intervene collectively against Israel, perhaps under the Tripartite Declaration, if operations were begun in Sinai, was deeply disturbing to the Israeli government. Earlier that afternoon it had taken the decision that at least a limited operation should be launched against Egypt.

On Monday, October 29, the Israeli Cabinet reconsidered its decisions of the previous day, in continuation of Sunday's meeting, and decided "to review the scope of the operation in a day or so." During that day, the American, British, and French ambassadors all paid visits to Mrs. Golda Meir, the foreign minister, asking for an explanation of Israel's mobilization and troop movements. The French ambassador expressed his government's "deep concern at the gravity of the situation which might develop." That evening an airborne battalion was dropped by parachute near Mitla "without incident."

News of the operation reached the prime minister in his darkened sick-room an hour later, at ten minutes past six. On the following morning, Tuesday, October 30, he got the news that Egyptian aircraft had attacked Israel's ground forces. This permitted him to review his previous orders (explained in the next chapter) that no Israeli aircraft were to attack Egyptian troops or Egyptian aircraft, unless the latter had attacked first, and he informed the commander of Israel's Air Force that operations in support of ground forces could begin at one o'clock that afternoon.

That same Tuesday evening Britain announced on the radio that she was sending an ultimatum to both Israel and Egypt, demanding that the troops of both countries should keep clear of the Suez Canal, and that an area extending to ten miles on each side of it should, in effect, be demilitarized. Israel's Cabinet remained in session until midnight, when the precise terms of the ultimatum were received from the Israel Embassy in London. The Israel Cabinet then spent another hour or so deciding its reply. When it had been sent—accepting the ultimatum—Israel's General Headquarters was required to make an immediate report on the effects of this acceptance on the plans of campaign.

That phrase "plans of campaign" (in the plural) is significant. In the next chapter I shall try to show that alternative plans existed, that the scope of the operations was not determined in advance, and that General Headquarters sought to retain freedom of action to diminish or increase the scope until the morning of Wednesday, October 31. For the moment, however, I am concerned not with the actual plans, but with what happened on the military levels below General Headquarters during the hundred hours of mobilization that preceded the start of operations. In order to do so, I must describe briefly my own personal movements.

Before the project of this book was even approved, I had the opportunity of driving along the central road through Sinai by way of El Auja on the frontier, Abu Aweigila, and Bir Gifgafa to the point close to the canal, and opposite Ismailia, where the Israeli troops had halted in response to the British ultimatum. We got there on the evening of Tuesday, November 6, exactly eight days after the operations had begun. By then, most of the Egyptian tanks and transport which could still be made serviceable had been driven, towed, or transported back to Israel. But the vast clutter of derelicts that remained on the sites of the various battles, and all along the route, were evidence of a campaign carried out at lightning speed which, I concluded, could have been made possible only by the most careful and detailed planning and preparation in all departments and on all levels.

This conclusion was confirmed during the first two days of my research, which Danny and I spent in Israel's War Office. It was plain to us, from our conversations with the heads of the various departments, that the planning of the campaign had been both detailed and expert. But there was one notable exception.

It was obvious that the most difficult and vital part of the whole campaign had been, not the fighting itself, but the mobilization. This was mainly the responsibility of the quartermaster general. It was therefore surprising to learn from him that he had been at the Senior Officers' School in Devizes, Wiltshire, England, at the time when mobilization started, and that he was not recalled to Israel until the process was finished and the operations were about to start. Our conclusion at the time was that it must be a pretty good department that could exercise full-scale mobilization when its chief was out of the country. It did not occur to us until the next day that the whole operation might have been unpremeditated and undertaken only on the spur of the moment.

The next day Danny took me down to Southern Command Headquarters for the first of our visits outside Tel Aviv. We were led into the war room, where we met the heads of the various staff sections. After a few minutes I had to interrupt. The chief staff officer of the G (or Operations) Section had said, "We got our warning order giving us the order of battle and the objects of the campaign on the afternoon of October twenty-sixth."

This was just not possible. Southern Command was in charge of all operations in the Sinai Campaign. If it had known nothing about it until October 26, it could have been given only three days for planning and preparation before the actual operations started. Since this seemed impossible, it was clear at once that Southern Command must have prepared its plans for the Sinai Campaign a long time in advance. The staff must have been all ready to put them into effect. All that it had to do, when it got the warning order, was open the relevant filing cabinet and take out the appropriate files, which would have contained all the necessary orders.

"I was left gasping," said the head of G Section, "at the idea of a full-scale campaign to take the Sinai Peninsula. Until that moment, I had never considered operations in terms of anything greater than a full-scale reprisal raid entailing forces of brigade size or less."

"It was the most fantastic headache," said the chief signals officer. "Our signals had never done an exercise entailing communications for more than a couple of brigades. We hadn't got the men or the equipment for anything bigger. We hadn't even got the electrical accumulators, which were all in store. It takes eight days to 'initial-charge' accumulators. It was lucky that we were able to find a way of dry-charging them in eight hours."

"It just wasn't on," the head of Q Department told me. (He had served for a long time in the British Army and was well accustomed to its jargon.) "We had never contemplated the movement into the area of more than a couple of brigades. Now we were required, at three days' notice—*three days'*, mark you!—to dispose many times this number of troops. If you look at the map, the roads simply don't exist. Nor do the necessary police and movements staff. And where on earth could we find all that number of assembly areas, sites for dumps, and water points?"

A posse of staff officers, all of us—including Danny, the Staff College instructor—asked ourselves how long we would need, theoretically, to make the minimum plans and preparations necessary to concentrate and supply these forces, let alone to send them into action. We worked it out silently, and each of us scribbled a figure on a scrap of paper. We were all agreed that, working day and night, we might have done the staff work in three weeks. It had been done in three days.

It then occurred to me that everyone was pulling my leg; or that they had been told by General Headquarters, for some obscure reason, that I was to be hoodwinked in this particular respect. But as the conference continued, extending to four or five hours interspersed with refreshment, and as it disintegrated into interludes for personal recollection and the discovery of all sorts of past occasions and experiences which I had in common with various members of the staff, this possibility collapsed. You cannot continue, for more than a few minutes, let alone a few hours, to hoodwink a technical colleague. And I had spent three or four years of war doing the same kind of job as the rest of them.

"To say that traffic control was a pain in the neck," said "Q," "would be an understatement. We had only got two possible roads for concentrating this force. They could only be used by night. In two nights, several thousand vehicles had to be moved down these two roads. They traveled at an average speed of twenty miles an hour, and an average density of nearly a hundred vehicles to the mile. Honestly, I don't know how we did it," said "Q." "The great majority of vehicles were requisitioned civilian trucks, many of them with civilian drivers. And no vehicle in our Army has any identification mark to connect it with its unit." Danny and I agreed that any staff officer in the world would tell you that it could not be done.

"It worked," said "G," "simply because we couldn't use the book. We had to throw away the book and improvise." Israel's Army is trained to improvise and to use individual initiative right through all ranks. Provided the unit or sub-unit, or even the individual driver, had been told exactly where he had to go, he somehow got there.

I thought I saw the answer. True, Southern Command had had no warning, but plans and preparations must have been made at a lower level of command, so that only Southern Command had to be brought into the picture at the last moment. This theory turned out to be equally false. The formation used in this campaign was the brigade; and when a large-scale operation is to be undertaken, a number of brigades are grouped under a task-force headquarters. And although these task-force headquarters are permanently established, and fully trained, I was soon to learn that they, like the staff of Southern Command, had had no previous warning of the Sinai Campaign, or indeed of any large-scale adventures. And when I got down to the level of brigade commanders, nearly all of whom I met personally, I was to learn that they were equally unprepared, not only for this particular campaign, but for any operations of anything like these dimensions. When I come to recount the movements and engagements of these various brigades, it will be noted that none of them received any warning until the night of October 25, and that few of them were warned until nearly twenty-four hours later.

I think that these facts are relevant to the issue of collusion. Surely collusion would imply some degree of deliberation, premeditation, advance preparation, and even operational cooperation? Yet—as will be apparent later—there was no cooperation whatsoever between the Navies, Armies, and Air Forces of Israel on the one hand and of Britain and France on the other. And if there was any premeditation or preparation in Israel, its grotesque inefficiency contrasts very strangely with the extreme efficiency with which the campaign itself was conducted.

In fact, the campaign was undertaken at a time which was most unfortunate for Israel's Air Force (this is explained in Chapter IX) and when the size of Israel's Army under arms was at its minimum. The quartermaster general who was responsible for mobilization was out of the country. No plans or preparations of any sort had been made on any military level lower than General Headquarters. The fact that General Headquarters had prepared these plans in advance—and presumably plans for every conceivable kind of operation on every frontier—is evidence only that it is not grossly incompetent. One of the principal jobs of every general headquarters of every army is to prepare plans against any possible contingency.

It may seem impossible that a campaign conducted with such extraordinary competence could have been mounted only on the spur of the moment, but the conversations that I had at Southern Command, and everything that I discovered thereafter, convinced us that, impossible or not, it was the truth. The "spur" was the increasing strangulation of the economic blockade, the mounting tension of the fedayeen activities, and the obvious preparations for invasion by Egypt, whose prospects of success had been so much enhanced by the establishment of the Unified Command of Arab States, and whose Army had received such formidable reinforcements from Russian arms, Russian instructors, and—it was conjectured—Russian promises. I do not know whether or not Russia's preoccupation with Hungary was any part of that "spur." But I should guess it was.

IV

The Plan

THIS chapter deals with the plan for the Sinai Campaign as it stood in Israel's General Headquarters at the time when the operation was mounted. A plan is the product of a great deal of study leading to the production of a staff study—an "appreciation" in British military jargon or an "estimate" in American. I have not seen any of the planning papers or studies at Israel's General Headquarters; but I have had the plan explained to me in detail by the heads of several Israeli War Office departments.

The staff studies (or appreciations or estimates) which precede a plan must take into account all the factors which influence the achievement of a stated "object." Israel's object in taking warlike action against Egypt at the end of October 1956 was quite simply to put an end to "all that"—"all that" being the load of exasperation described in Chapter II. It meant, for a start, forestalling the Egyptian offensive that was being prepared in the highly fortified Gaza Strip, in the vast dumps of Iron Curtain equipment close to the frontier at El Arish, in the "firm base" which had been established and fortified at Abu Aweigila, close to the frontier on the central axis of Sinai, and in the new or improved airfields, which could have nothing but an aggressive purpose, in that same central sector along the road from Ismailia and at El Arish. It also meant putting an end to the fedayeen activities, whose source was the Egyptian Army in Sinai and Gaza. And it meant, further, the open-

The Plan

ing of the Gulf of Aqaba and the port of Elath to the legitimate traffic of Israel's shipping. It meant, finally, putting an end to Egypt's illegal blockade in the Suez Canal.

The way to end all these aggravations was not to capture the Sinai Peninsula, but decisively to defeat the Egyptian Army. Nobody wants Sinai for itself. Apart from a few small, almost negligible oil wells on the eastern shores of the Gulf of Suez, and a manganese mine, the Sinai Peninsula is economically valueless. The place is virtually uninhabited, except for a very few fishermen along the coast and a considerable number of nomadic Bedouin who certainly hate Egypt and the Egyptians as much as they do Israel—or indeed anybody else. The only use of the Sinai Peninsula to either Egypt or Israel was, and still is, strategic. Sinai is the area in which either country can best defend its frontiers, and from which either country can best act offensively against the other. But at the end of October 1956 it was in Sinai that the Egyptian Army could be defeated.

Yet even the defeat of the Egyptian Army was not an end in itself. It was only a step toward the negotiation of peace: the peace that Israel had been trying for eight years to extract from her armistice agreements with the Arab countries. General Dayan explained to me, "The Egyptians had to know in their hearts, and our other Arab neighbors to know also, that they could not defeat Israel." This was the negative aspect of the operations. But they also had a positive side to them. Dayan said, "We have to persuade Egypt and our other neighbors that we are a country that they can live alongside."

From the negative point of view, Israel had to repeat the defeat which she had inflicted on the Egyptians' invading Army in 1948. As Dayan said, "Surely two defeats in eight years must have some effect?" From the positive point of view, Israel had to conduct her operations as cleanly and humanely as possible. As Dayan said, "We did not want to kill a lot of Egyptians." He added, "There are forty million Arabs, so what's the use of killing five thousand, ten

No one wanted to kill Egyptians or take them prisoner

thousand, fifteen thousand of them? It was not even vital to destroy or take their equipment. They could always get more from Russia. What mattered was their defeat."

Nor was there any point in taking a lot of Egyptian prisoners. "Let them run away!" Dayan said. And as for their officers: "They are no good anyway. Much better to leave them where they are in their Army, than for them to be replaced by younger men who might be better." Several times Dayan repeated that nobody had wanted to inflict casualties on the Egyptians as an end in itself. "But if we could save fifty Israeli casualties—that was another matter." This, then, was Israel's object in taking warlike action against Egypt: to achieve victory for its own sake, and to do so at the minimum possible cost in terms of Israeli casualties.

There are of course a great many factors which affect the achievement of an object in any military campaign. Three of these factors, with which I must deal specifically, are the nature of the terrain, the comparative strengths of the two armies—in terms of numbers, equipment, deployment, training, morale, and temperament—and the political consequences. For a start, I had better try to describe the Sinai Peninsula.

When, on November 6, 1956, I first drove along the road that runs from Beersheba to Ismailia—a road familiar to very many British and Commonwealth soldiers of two world wars—I wrote in my notebook, "The Sinai desert is 24,000 square miles of absolutely nothing. Nobody lives there, or could. You can drive for a hundred miles without seeing anyone except soldiers from somewhere else. No tree or even scrub; nothing but flat sand on which a Piper Cub can land almost anywhere; and sometimes rolling seas of sand, or a range of sand hills perpetually changing shape; and in places fierce rock. No bird or beast, except one stray dog in search of a master and finding only an Egyptian corpse, missed by the burial parties, beside which he lay down and wept."

This little gem of descriptive writing was not very apt. It applies more or less to the central sector of Sinai, through which we were driving that day. But during the course of the next three weeks, while I was still exploring the place, sometimes by car, in parts by jeep, and otherwise from a Piper Cub, I relearned the old, old lesson of my youth that a desert is rarely deserted. When surprised from the air, the Bedouin are liable to be seen appearing from nowhere and, almost instantly, disappearing again into nothing, leaving behind them only a black-robed girl and a scurry of black goats clustering in fear of the aircraft round their solitary protectress.

These Bedouin can be extremely dangerous to anybody, no matter who he is. Their local sport, and sometimes their livelihood, depends on cutting your throat for the sake of your socks, let alone your wrist watch. At the same time they observe the strictest code of desert hospitality, which demands that if you go to their tents and put yourself under their protection with the formal declaration,

"*Anna dakhilak,*" they must not only take you in, but also defend you with their lives. The difficulty is to get to their tents before they get you on their playing fields; and many Egyptian soldiers who were wandering homeward from battle failed to do so.

From the air, moreover, you can see that in times past there have been many areas of intensive cultivation. The marks of ancient terraces, tillages, and enclosures show that there must be water here, which has latterly been lost. And even in comparatively recent times, during periods of British administration, measures were taken to preserve rainfall by building dams across the wadis, whereby fertility was brought to remote places.

It is only the upper half of the peninsula that is desert in the proper sense. If you draw a line obliquely across the map from Elath, at the top of the Gulf of Aqaba, to Ras al Sudr, on the Gulf of Suez, everything below it is hilly or mountainous. The farther south you go, the higher the mountains, until in the area of Mount Sinai they rise in strange, dreamlike or moonlike shapes to 9000 feet.

Along the northern or Mediterranean coast of the peninsula there is a coastal strip with water in many places. And down the western coast, which is the eastern shore of the Gulf of Suez, leading into the Red Sea, the coastal area has a few oil wells and a manganese mine, in addition to water. Around the tip itself, as you fly from the Gulf of Suez into the Gulf of Aqaba, there is quite a broad sandy plain, until you have turned the corner and come to Sharm el Sheikh and Ras Nasrani, the two newly fortified villages by which Egypt had closed the Gulf to Israel's shipping.

At various times in history, Sinai has been a kind of transit camp, a meeting place for those who were traveling the trade routes between the Tigris and the Euphrates on the east, and the civilizations of the Nile on the west. Here two cultures mingled, the Babylonian and the Egyptian, and two races met, the Semite and the Ham-African.

In southern Sinai there has been found the earliest record of

The Plan

alphabetical writing carved in stone; and in the north, in areas where wells are still more numerous, there are the prehistoric remains of the early Stone Age. Thousands of years after that age, in the days of Abraham, Isaac, and Jacob, there were static settlements in Sinai around the main routes. And after the Exodus, when the children of Israel were traveling in the "wilderness of Sin," they met various Semitic tribes, such as the Midianites. This was in the south. And again in the south, the traces of Egyptian settlements date back to 3000 B.C., around the mines where copper and turquoise were got. And here on the Holy Mount, Moses was given the Law. Scholars argue vehemently as to whether it was here or somewhere quite different; but traditionally it is Jebel Musa (Mount of Moses), a peak which is over 7000 feet high, in the middle of that massive red range of granite and sandstone near the southern tip.

During the Hellenic and Roman eras, the point of gravity of civilization moved to southern Europe, and Sinai had only a local importance as a highway between Egypt and Palestine until, with the opening of the Suez Canal, it was restored to more general use. Yet for the last two thousand years hermits have lived there. And many religious sects have sent a constant trickle of pilgrims to the traditional source of the Jewish, Christian, and Moslem faiths. Here there stands, at the foot of Jebel Musa, the Monastery of St. Catherine, which was built in 520 A.D. by Justinian. Here there is water, and here grow trees and crops. And for centuries the monks have fed the Bedouin with bread and, in return, have had their protection.

When the hostilities were over and Moshe Dayan went to visit the monastery, it is said that he was hoisted up the wall in a cradle by ropes, and was met at the top by twelve monks in black robes waiting in the central courtyard. They said to him, "We know that you are Israelis and have conquered Sinai. You are the first Israelis to come here." And they served Dayan and his soldiers with coffee and pears. Maybe the glamour of this military pilgrimage was slightly tarnished when Dayan was told that Cecil B. de Mille had brought his cameras there when shooting his film *The Ten Commandments*.

For three hundred years the Turks ruled Sinai until, in the 1880s, after the Suez Canal had been built, the British, French, and Russians gave it to Mohammed Ali (then in power in Egypt), as part of the bargain by which political boundaries were fixed. On the eve of World War I, the British handed Sinai to Egypt, with the border line running in a straight line from Rafa in the north, to Taba, at the top of the Gulf of Aqaba, in the south.

There are three lateral routes running across the Sinai Peninsula from east to west—that is to say, from Israel to Egypt. The northern route, which follows the coast, goes through Gaza and El Arish to Qantara; the central route from Beersheba to Ismailia; and the southern route from Kuntilla—which is on the Egyptian side of the Negev frontier—through El Thamed, Nakhl, and the Mitla Passes. Between the northern and central routes there is an important road running from El Arish to Abu Aweigila, with a fork to Gebel Libni.

Joining the central to the southern routes there are a number of roads or tracks which are important to the story, notably one leading southwards from Kuseima to Nakhl, and another, more westward track running due south from Gebel Libni, through Bir Hasana, also to Nakhl. In addition, there is a perfectly good track, which is not marked on the ordinary maps, running southwards from Bir Gifgafa to the road that joins Bir Hasana and the Mitla Passes.

There are two other roads which concern us; they run, respectively and approximately, down the west and east coasts of the peninsula. So far as quality is concerned, they look the same on the ordinary maps; but whereas the one along the Gulf of Suez has an excellent surface, and has recently been extended by the Egyptians for some eighty miles to their fortifications at Sharm el Sheikh, the one running down the Gulf of Aqaba is little better than

The Plan

a mule-track and, in places, worse. On most maps there is shown a network of tracks running from east to west across the bottom third of the peninsula. These are not there at all.

I had better say at once that, even allowing for cartographer's license in the Middle East, the roads that are shown on most maps of Sinai are not what anybody might expect. Sometimes they are tarred and metaled affairs on which an ordinary car can drive at high speed for long distances; sometimes they are tracks which are negotiable by wheeled vehicles; sometimes they are simply a strip of relatively flat country on which a camel can plod with comfort, while a jeep may or may not get stuck; and sometimes they simply do not exist. It is for this reason that I have taken time to indicate here those roads or tracks that are important to the story of the campaign.

The next factor to be considered is the relative strengths of the two armies. The Egyptian Army consisted of approximately four divisions, or ten brigades. Of these, three were armored, although one of them was only in the process of being equipped and organized. To the east of the canal there was the 8th Division in the Gaza area, and the 3rd Division deployed between El Arish and Abu Aweigila. In addition, there was the Light Mobile Frontier Force, or Desert Frontier Force, equipped mainly with armored jeeps and troop carriers, formerly a camel corps, but now mechanized.

There were three kinds of Egyptian formations in existence. The regular division (for instance, 3rd Division) was on the British pattern with three infantry brigades, supporting artillery, and usually a tank battalion. These were composed of Egyptian conscripts with regular officers and a nucleus of regular other-ranks. Next, there was a division (8th Division) composed of a Palestinian brigade, recruited in Gaza and organized on the same pattern as a regular brigade, with which a brigade of National Guard was coupled. And finally, there were these National Guard brigades, which were of reduced strength and manned by volunteers who protested fanatical fervor, but whose main motive for enlisting was probably cash.

The Egyptian forces in the Sinai Peninsula amounted to approximately 45,000 men, all of them deployed in positions which were formidably prepared for defense. Israel put against them a force of approximately the same size. Technically speaking, the Egyptians had the superior equipment. The Russian T.34 medium tank is better than the Israeli Sherman or even the Super-Sherman. It has wider tracks, which make it particularly suitable for soft sand, and its gun has a longer range and fires a heavier shell.

Equally, the Russian SU 100 tank-destroyer, with which the Egyptian Army was equipped, had a heavier gun than that of the French AMX of the Israeli Army, and was equally maneuverable. The British "Archer" anti-tank gun and the Russian (or Czech) 57 mm. were both good weapons, held in large numbers by Egypt, and should have been adequate against Israel's Shermans.

So far as the Air Forces were concerned, Egypt had a distinct numerical superiority in jet aircraft. On the other hand, the spear of her fighter force, the Russian MIG 15, was not the equal of Israel's best fighter aircraft, the French Mystère. And also, although Egypt had more MIG 15s than Israel had Mystères, she had fewer pilots. On the other hand, Egypt had at least 50 of the most modern medium bombers, the Russian Ilyushin 28, whereas Israel had none at all.

This deficiency of bombers was a secret that was not very closely guarded. Dayan, at a press conference, was questioned by a reporter who, hoping to prove "collusion," asked, "If you did not know that the British and French were going to bomb the Egyptian airfields, why then didn't you do so yourself during the two days before the Anglo-French bombing began?" Standing before a battery of cameras, arc lights, and microphones, Dayan looked discomfited. He fingered his black eye-patch; he scratched the crown of his head where there is a slightly bald patch. Then he turned to his director of military intelligence, a dark, high-strung young man who was sitting morosely behind him, and asked, "Can I trust them? Dare I tell them off the record?" The young man did not answer; and Dayan, turning back to his audience of reporters, stepped to the front of the platform. "Gentlemen," he said in a low voice or a loud whisper, "in strict confidence I will tell you why we did not bomb the Egyptian airfields. . . . We have no bombers."

After this diversion, which concludes the comparison of Israeli and Egyptian equipment, I must return to the deployment of the Egyptian forces in Sinai. Their German advisers had proposed to them that the major defenses should be sited in the western part of the peninsula, some sixty miles to the east of the canal, on the uplands which run from north to south in the area of Bir Gifgafa. From this area both the northern and the southern lateral roads across the peninsula could be controlled; and for this reason, it was ground vital to either a defending or an attacking army.

Since there is nothing to the east of the Bir Gifgafa area which is of any value whatsoever to anyone, the German recommendations were sound. Nasser rejected them for three reasons. First, he did not expect to be attacked and was not concerned with defense: he wanted his main positions and bases to be as close as possible to the Israel frontier, to serve as a springboard for his own invasion. Second, his prestige might suffer from the military abandonment of either his frontier or the Gaza Strip, and it is on prestige that any dictator depends for survival. And third, the fedayeen bases and headquarters in the Gaza Strip had to be defended and supplied from Egypt.

Accordingly, the main Egyptian defenses were based on the triangle of Rafa–El Arish–Abu Aweigila. This will henceforward be known simply as the Triangle. To man the Triangle, Egypt had her 3rd Infantry Division, while the 8th Division was next door in the Gaza area. Apart from the Triangle, there were two areas on the southern road that were of great natural strength and were heavily fortified: Kuntilla, near the frontier, and El Thamed, some forty miles to the southwest. On the Gulf of Aqaba, in Ras Nasrani and Sharm el Sheikh, the Egyptian garrison of over 2000 men were in positions of immense strength, and were provisioned for a period of many months. They ought to have been able to hold up any force for an indefinite period.

The main problem of the Israeli planners was to assess the fighting potential of the Egyptian Army. Had it substantially improved since 1948 when Israel had last defeated it? Had the German and Russian instructors, and the mass of modern weapons and equipment, turned it into a much better fighting machine than before? The Israeli planners were inclined to think not.

The Egyptian Army, like Israel's Army, is composed mainly of conscripts. The Egyptian conscript is either a *fellah*—that is to say, a farm laborer or peasant—or a townsman. There are very many remissions from national service, since a large proportion of the *fellaheen* suffer from various forms of sickness, of which malaria, eye diseases, and bilharzia are the most common; and a large number of the townsmen have venereal infections.

The fellah is normally illiterate, is not interested in fighting, and is so subject to privation and oppression that he is not really military material in any normal sense. The townsmen can mostly read or write. Therefore they comprise the NCO class in the Army. The Egyptian NCO is not usually a man who has any special military qualifications or aptitude for leadership, but one who is approximately literate.

The Egyptian officer comes from a family which is prosperous or has influence or is of some social standing. Young men of this class have been educated at a secondary school, from which they graduate into their father's business, or to a university, or to the Officers' School. The lure of the Officers' School is considerable, since Nasser has been at pains to sponsor the officer class or caste. It is well paid and has considerable social status.

The course at the Officers' School lasts three years, and the syllabus comprises a mass of theory. Theoretically, the Egyptian officer is a better-educated soldier than the Israeli. Also, he has been implanted with a great deal of technical training, so that he knows his weapons in minute detail. True, he has also been taught leadership; but you cannot lead a man whom you have learned from infancy to despise. When the military commander of Sharm el Sheikh, Lieutenant Colonel Khana Neguib, was captured and was asked to explain the moderation of his resistance to the Israeli attack, he gave three reasons. The last and most important was, in his own words, "Point three—my men are no good."

The fellah fears his officer, who comes from a class which has power over him and is far above him socially and economically. When a group of Egyptian officers and soldiers were taken prisoners, the latter usually turned their backs on their officers and declined to speak to them. At El Arish, when an Egyptian officer was charged with issuing water to a group of his own men who were ravaged by thirst, he rushed to the water point himself, and had started to drink when he was torn aside, and almost torn to bits, by his own troops. An Israeli NCO (of Oriental origin) took charge of the proceedings, and the Egyptian soldiers followed his instructions in an orderly and well disciplined manner.

Usually the Egyptian officer has no liking for the countryside and no connection with it. By birth and upbringing he is a townsman and, despite his lengthy training and martial attitude, his thoughts and interests attach him primarily to the cafés and women of Cairo. In all his deepest feelings he detests the desert. When a senior Egyptian officer was being interrogated and was asked why he had so readily abandoned his position, he answered with passion, "What do *I* want with this desert?"

An Egyptian frequently has a way of telling lies in order to justify his actions, and, once these lies have been told, he comes to believe them. A company commander who wanted permission to withdraw from one of his Abu Aweigila positions reported that he was being attacked by overwhelming forces. His battalion commander, in speaking to brigade, translated these forces into "more than a battalion." By the time the information got to General Headquarters in Cairo, the attacking force had grown to "at least a brigade." In fact it was a single Israeli jeep which had lost its way and had no intention, at that time, of attacking anyone.

An Egyptian platoon commander who had been in charge of a number of Archers—an Archer is the British Valentine tank mounted with an anti-tank seventeen-pounder—which were dug into a ridge at Abu Aweigila, was asked why, when abandoning his guns, he had not even spiked them. He insisted that he had done so; he really believed it. And when he was taken back to his own guns and shown them intact and in perfect fighting order, he could not understand it. Of course they had been spiked; he had told somebody to do it.

The insertion into the Egyptian Army of any number of Russian or German instructors, or even active officers or NCOs, is unlikely to be effective. Nobody and nothing can change the Egyptian soldier except a social and economic revolution in Egypt. No first-rate instructor can do more than teach the fellah to do one simple task by rote.

If you care to compare the Egyptian Army with the Arab Legion, you must remember two things. First, the Legionnaire was trained and led by British officers for fifteen or twenty years. Secondly, the Legionnaire was either a Bedouin or a hill man. In either case, his upbringing from childhood tended to make him military material. He had owned his own rifle. He knew by instinct how to use ground. He had to be taught only, or mainly, how to fight collectively in an organized unit. The fellah from the plains lacked this advantage.

Nevertheless, the Egyptian fellah will fight bravely in certain circumstances. If he is cornered and cannot get away, he will sometimes defend himself with courage and resolution, rather than surrender. He will man his weapon competently against an advancing enemy so long as he is well established and is on familiar ground. If he is given time to fight defensively, he will do so. Hence, he will put up a much better opposition against a carefully prepared, deliberate attack than against Israel's unorthodox tactics. When the Egyptian soldier has been rushed or surprised, or when his positions have once been penetrated, he is usually stricken with panic. Then, unless he is cornered, he will seek to escape.

The Plan

The Israeli planners were not so cocksure about the fighting inefficiency of the Egyptian Army as I may have suggested. Nevertheless it is important to recognize that their plan was based on an accurate assessment of the Egyptian Army. If the enemy had been better, the plan would not have been the same; nor the tactics. Against more resolute and steadier troops the tactics employed by Israel in Sinai would have meant, not spectacular successes, but bloody disasters.

The political factor which must have influenced the planners had three main aspects. First, the question had to be asked—what sort of war was this to be? Was it to be total war which might develop into world war; or was it to be localized war on the Korean pattern? Total war would mean air attacks on military installations, and such action usually develops, in due course, into air attacks on civilian centers of population. A limited or localized war would leave the respective air forces more or less out of it. It must be remembered that no air power had ever been used by Israel in the course of her reprisal raids, a decision which had always been disputed by the Israel Air Force. After all, the Air Force used to argue, it could achieve a great deal more, with much less loss, by sending a few aircraft with a few bombs and rockets than could a military force sent across the frontier to capture fedayeen headquarters in a police station, evacuate its occupants, and blow up the place as a gesture.

In fact, Israel started the Sinai Campaign with a code of aerial warfare that was more strict than that of the "Yalu River rules" of the Korean War. The canal was the equivalent of the Yalu River, and to the west of it lay sanctuary for Egyptian air and ground forces. Aircraft were not allowed to reconnoiter across the canal; nor to attack enemy aircraft, unless the enemy aircraft had first taken hostile action; nor to attack Egyptian ground forces until Israel's ground forces had first been attacked from the air by Egypt.

By imposing upon herself these rules, Israel handed the air initiative to Egypt on a plate. It was a political bridle and bearing-rein put on Israel's Air Force, the more severe because of Egypt's numerical superiority in air power. It meant, at the very least, that the plan for Israel's ground forces must be based on the assumption that the enemy would have some measure of air superiority over the battlefields. It was on this assumption that the plan was in fact based—which is perhaps another piece of evidence against the charge of collusion. If Israel had made her plan on the expectation of Anglo-French intervention, she could have assumed her own air superiority and might have acted very differently at the start.

A second aspect of the political factor was the question—how would Israel's other neighbors react to her hostile action against Egypt? They had long been allies and fellow members of the Arab League, and had fervently protested their unity, at least where "Jewish-occupied Palestine" was concerned. Their alliance had been immensely strengthened—or so it seemed—by the establishment of the Unified Command of Arab States. And although Israel was undoubtedly capable of taking on all her Arab neighbors simultaneously, as she had done before in 1948 under far more adverse circumstances, it would mean a full-scale and costly war, as apart from a campaign. She did not desire to defeat her Arab neighbors either jointly or severally; she wanted a victory over their leader, Egypt, which might influence all the Arab states to agree to negotiate peace.

The main hope of defeating Egypt, without her allies' intervening, was to do so before they could in fact intervene with any prospect of success. If the chances of success looked good, they would undoubtedly invade Israel, or try to; if the chances looked poor, they would undoubtedly keep out of it. Therefore, whatever Israel did must be done quickly and must produce quick results. In addition, it must take Egypt's allies by surprise and present them with a situation which they had not expected, and which they could not turn to profit at Israel's expense.

The third feature of the political factor was, in my opinion—and this is only my guesswork—a degree of uncertainty and apprehension, on the part of Israel, about the way the world would

The Plan

react to the start of her operations. If the great powers, or some of them, would see the thing as Israel saw it, if they would recognize that Egypt had always insisted that she was at war with Israel, and that she had taken all sorts of warlike measures against Israel short of invasion, and that she was preparing to launch an actual invasion in the near future, then Israel could count on being let alone to carry out a full-scale campaign and win a decisive victory.

But if the great powers, which in the past had been so blind to Israel's plight, were to denounce Israel's first moves as "unprovoked aggression," and were themselves to take action to restrain her, then she might feel herself compelled to curtail her operations. In brief, she wanted to retain freedom of action to determine the scope of her operations at some stage after the operations had actually started. This conjecture is supported by the decision of the Israeli Cabinet on Monday, October 29, the day on which the operations began, "to review the scope of the operation in a day or so."

We can now add up the factors that influenced the plan. The object was victory for its own sake. There was, however, a chance that this might be denied to Israel, either by the intervention of one or more of the great powers, or by some other factor which had not been predicted. For instance, the Egyptian Army might prove to be more formidable than had been anticipated, or the reaction of the Egyptian Air Force might be so effective that to continue the operation would be too costly.

Hence, if it should happen that, on some account or other, Israel should be denied the complete victory that she sought, she must at least make sure of some tangible success. For many reasons —amongst them the morale of her own people and the effect on her Arab neighbors—she must at least secure an imposing prize. A suitable prize would be the liquidation of Egyptian forces in the Gaza Strip, whence their fedayeen activities were being launched; or the opening of the Gulf of Aqaba to Israel's shipping by the capture of Ras Nasrani and Sharm el Sheikh. The great powers might protest, but they could not very well take action to prevent Israel from destroying the fedayeen bases in the Gaza Strip. Nor could they reasonably condemn her for seeking, by capturing Sharm el Sheikh, to end the Egyptian blockade which was itself illegal and a warlike act.

The ideal plan would provide for the winning of these prizes as steps toward complete victory. At the same time, it would be phased in such a way that, after the initial action, there would be a pause during which the Israeli government could "review the scope of the operation."

It was not very easy to prepare a plan on this basis. Certainly Israel could be sure of liquidating the Egyptian forces in the Gaza Strip; but she could not hope to be allowed by the great powers to stay there, nor could this stroke be a step toward the defeat of the Egyptian Army. Its ultimate effect in military terms might even be adverse. It would be a slow and deliberate, rather than a sudden and speedy, action; and it would give Egypt and her allies time to gather themselves together, under their Unified Command, to make a coordinated response.

Nor was the capture of Sharm el Sheikh an easy project as an isolated operation. It is doubtful if it was even feasible. The place was very heavily fortified and garrisoned. The only road that led to it ran down the Gulf of Suez and, at its nearest point, was 150 miles from Israel's frontier. The track, or mule-track, down the eastern coast of the peninsula was, in fact, traversed by an Israeli brigade. But this was not attempted until the rest of the Egyptian Army was preoccupied elsewhere.

Since neither Gaza nor Sharm el Sheikh were suitable targets for attack in the first instance, the planners had to find some other way of opening the proceedings. They must devise some bold and imaginative stroke which would be bound to provoke reaction from Egypt. They could then wait and see how Egypt and the world responded, and proceed to meet that response. It was like passing the service to the other side—but doing so with the confidence that the other side was incapable of delivering a service that could not be returned decisively.

The opening stroke chosen by the planners was to drop a battalion of an airborne brigade in the Mitla area, and to reinforce it overland as speedily as possible. The spot chosen for the drop—on the eastern side of the Mitla Passes—was only forty miles from Suez, and the same distance from a major Egyptian airfield at Shallufa. It was a step that was bound to provoke reaction by Egypt; but the reaction would be delayed by the fact that there is no bridge at Suez, and that Egyptian reinforcements would have to come across the canal by ferry. By the time that they had done so, it was hoped that the Mitla Passes would be in Israel's hands, and that the Israeli forces would be established 25 miles from Suez itself, and a little less from the coastal road that led down the Gulf of Suez to Sharm el Sheikh.

The drop at Mitla would be followed by a twenty-four-hour pause, during which no further military action would be taken except by those troops that were to reinforce the parachute battalion. This pause would provide Israel with the chance to "review the scope of her operations." She could, if necessary, decide to go no farther and let the Mitla affair appear to be just one more reprisal. Or, if she decided otherwise, she could expand the Mitla operation into a full-scale campaign.

The operations were planned in four phases to employ anything up to five independent forces:

Phase I: A parachute battalion would be dropped in the Mitla area at sunset on D-Day, October 29. At the same time, the remainder of that airborne brigade would cross the frontier to Kuntilla and advance with all possible speed to reinforce its parachute battalion. It would have to travel about 130 miles and, on the way, would have to take three strongly fortified positions at Kuntilla, El Thamed, and Nakhl, respectively. In case it got held up, a Central Task Force was to cross the frontier at Sabha, 60 miles to the north, and capture the road junction at Kuseima. From Kuseima this force could go to the help of the parachute battalion by way of Nakhl or, alternatively, by way of Bir Hasana.

Phase II: This was to be the twenty-four-hour pause. At the end of it, the decision would be taken what to do next. If it was decided to embark upon the full-scale campaign, there would follow:

Phase III: An independent force, the 9th Infantry Brigade, would make its way down the western shore of the Gulf of Aqaba to take Ras Nasrani and Sharm el Sheikh. If necessary, it would be assisted by forces from the Mitla area coming down the road along the Gulf of Suez and attacking Sharm el Sheikh in the rear. At the same time, the Central Task Force, part of which would already have taken Kuseima, would attack the Triangle at its Abu Aweigila apex; and a Northern Task Force would attack another apex of the Triangle at Rafa.

Phase IV: The Central Task Force, after taking Abu Aweigila, would exploit westward to the canal opposite Ismailia. The Northern Task Force, after taking Rafa, would take El Arish and exploit to the canal at Qantara. Once El Arish had fallen, the Gaza Strip would be sealed and, to use the military cliché that is customary in these cases, would "fall like a ripe plum." To help it do so, a fifth force, which would be kept in reserve during the first three phases, would attack Gaza from the East.

In the four chapters that follow, the operations of these various forces will be reported. Chapter V tells the story of the airborne brigade in the Mitla area. Chapter VI deals with the 9th Infantry Brigade, which took Sharm el Sheikh. Chapters VII and VIII deal, respectively, with the operations of the Central and Northern Task Forces in their attacks on the Triangle and in the subsequent exploitation of its capture. Chapter VIII deals also with the Gaza operation.

It is hard to say, even now, whether or not the operations went according to plan. It is equally hard to say whether or not the planners, in exceptionally difficult circumstances, evolved the best

They threw off their boots in order to travel lighter through the desert

possible plan—or even a very good one. Anybody can think of a dozen alternatives; and I dare say that, if any of those alternatives had been chosen as a substitute, the result would have been the same in the end.

At a cost of less than 180 men killed and 4 captured, Israel routed half the Egyptian Army. Something over 1000 were killed, and nearly 6000 were taken prisoners, of which only 202 were officers. The remarkably small proportion of officers amongst the prisoners is due to the fact that, in the Egyptian Army, it is an officer's privilege to be the first to run away.

This tally accounts for about 7000 of the 45,000 Egyptians who were in the Sinai Peninsula and the Gaza Strip at the start of operations. The Bedouin killed another 1000 and maybe many more, on their flight toward Egypt. The remainder got home without their equipment or personal arms, usually without their uniforms, and almost invariably without their boots. They threw away their boots in order to travel lighter through the desert. Not one Egyptian unit that was actually engaged in battle made an organized withdrawal to the canal. Those Egyptians that got home did so in small groups or as individuals. They had to travel cross-country, because Israel's armor was using the only two roads. Along these roads the Israeli Army had got to the canal—or rather, 10 miles short of it, in compliance with the British ultimatum—and established itself there within a hundred hours of the parachute drop at Mitla.

V

An Airborne Brigade in the South

PEOPLE who do jobs which are particularly hazardous are sometimes able to relax more profoundly than those who live steadier lives. I have often noticed this characteristic about such people as fighter and bomber pilots, men of the commandos and airborne troops. I noticed it again at the headquarters of an airborne brigade when they were telling me about the Mitla operations.

We were in the war room. Like any other war room's its walls were papered with maps, lit by fluorescent lights, and covered by discreet curtains when the maps were not in use. In the middle of the room there was a very large table; on the table, a litter of maps, orders, calculations and my notes. Superimposed upon this clutter, a quantity of refreshments, glasses of tea, squashy cakes, and what would be called, I suppose, "savory snacks." And lounging across the table, the commander of this airborne brigade, his intelligence officer, Danny, and myself.

The brigade commander was a very burly young man, a forceful enthusiast with a particularly wicked face. It had a full measure of military impudence to which had been added an even fuller measure of what the Israelis themselves call "Sabra cheek." He and his men had taken part in quite a number of reprisal raids during

"Shmual," the battalion commander who was always asleep

the past few years. Having long ago lost their amateur status, they were first-class professional soldiers who reckoned that fighting, rather than soldiering, was their job. They set about that job with artistry and zest. Afterward they discussed it with matter-of-fact enthusiasm as a tricky problem and its expert solution. In their red berets as they walk about the streets, the airborne troops show a well-mannered pride and smartness. Their physique is magnificent.

While the brigade commander talked, one of his battalion commanders—call him Shmual—a tall man with a beard and gentle blue eyes, contrived to lie full length in a chair designed for sitting erect. I felt that he needed only a leg rest to be settled for the night. One of the girls in uniform who was bringing us more tea— she was remarkably pretty—drew the same conclusion. As she went past, she gave a sideways kick at a second chair, pushing it across the floor toward Shmual, who, without opening his eyes, put his feet on it. Thus supine, he seemed to return absolutely to sleep; but now and again, in the course of narrative, a correction to what was being said issued murmurously from his lips.

"Our job," said the brigade commander—I will call him Dov, which is Hebrew for "bear"—"was to capture Nakhl junction and the Mitla Passes, and be prepared to exploit to the canal and move southward down the Gulf of Suez, and round the tip, to take part in the capture of Sharm el Sheikh."

Danny said, "Wait a moment! You remember what they told us? This operation only makes sense if you keep in mind that the whole Mitla affair was simply a means, the chosen means, of getting everything going. It was to be followed by that 'pause of twenty-four hours' that we talked about so much. We wanted, first of all, to see how the Egyptians would react." They could scarcely fail to react to the drop of a parachute battalion less than 40 miles from Suez, the same distance from one of their main fighter airfields, 180 miles from Israel's fighter airfields, and about 130 miles by road from Israel's frontier in the southern Negev. It seemed to me that the very craziness of this operation was one of its main features.

"We had to hurry," said Shmual with his eyes shut.

"Speed was the essence of the operation," said Danny. He has been almost over-trained at a British OCTU and in British units, and he uses these military clichés as readily as I do myself. But he was unquestionably right.

Speed was vital and, from the moment that this airborne brigade received its operation order, each hour might easily make the difference between a spectacular success and catastrophe. Once that parachute battalion had been dropped in the Mitla area, it would begin attracting to itself whatever Egyptian forces could be sent by ferry across the canal to dislodge it. It would probably be attacked by armored forces crossing from Ismailia to the central road, and turning south from Bir Gifgafa, where, although they are not marked on the ordinary maps, there are adequate tracks for both tanks and wheeled vehicles. Therefore the rest of that airborne brigade had to move with the utmost speed to reinforce its parachute battalion.

According to the plan, the whole brigade had to be in the Mitla area within 24 hours of the initial drop—that is to say, at the end of the "pause." To get there, it had first to capture three enemy positions, at Kuntilla, Thamed, and Nakhl, of which the first two were extremely strong, and the third quite formidable. At either Kuntilla or Thamed, both of which are sited on steep hills, a few resolute men could hold up an army for an almost indefinite period.

"And the roads were not good," Shmual said in his sleep. It was an understatement. At their best the roads were poor; in places they were appalling; at their worst—and there was plenty of worst —they did not exist.

"So we got our warning order on Thursday evening," Dov said.

"D minus four," said Danny.

"In the middle of a party," said Shmual.

"A party given specially for us," Dov said, "by the municipality of Ramat Gan. They have adopted us. Very nice; a very good party. I didn't see I should interrupt it. We were often getting these warning orders, on account of fedayeen or something of the sort. Usually they didn't turn into anything."

Toward midnight, when the party was going with a swing, the warning order was confirmed. It meant that something really was afoot. Discreetly, Dov extracted his battalion commanders. "I gave them two hours to cool their heads," he said; "then I told them at two o'clock in the morning; then I had to go to Southern Command Headquarters, and I was kept there till seven o'clock; then I came back and gave my own orders. That was Friday, nine o'clock at night."

"Nine-thirty," Shmual murmured.

"D minus three," said Danny.

Dov said, "I could only tell my own staff and the battalion commanders. The battalion commanders couldn't tell anyone, not their seconds-in-command, not their adjutants. It made difficulties."

"Extra work," Shmual said.

"Security was very strict," Danny said.

"So, all Saturday," Dov said, "the battalion commanders made their plans. I coordinated them at three o'clock in the afternoon."

"Three-thirty."

"D minus two."

Dov continued patiently. "The parachute battalion had to stay at base, of course, because of the Dakotas. So I did also, with one staff officer. The rest of the brigade moved that night to its concentration area. . . . Go on, Shmual!"

"A hundred miles," Shmual said, "to Ein Khussub."

"Ein Khussub!" I said. "Why Ein Khussub?" This tiny hamlet is on the wrong side of the Negev from Sinai. It is 70 miles from Giraffi in the middle of the Negev; and it is 50 miles from Giraffi to Suweilma, where the brigade was to cross the frontier. Why concentrate 120 miles, by road, away from your starting point? "Why Khussub?"

Dov asked a question in Hebrew. Danny answered. I think he said that it was all right. He explained. "Look! We were told at Southern Command that nobody was to know where the operation was to be. There you have it." I did indeed. Ein Khussub is on the Jordan frontier. Dov said, "Go on, Shmual!"

Shmual spoke better English than Dov, but I think the effort was too much for him. So Danny interpreted. And as I watched Shmual, relaxed, supine, and listened to his lazy Hebrew speech, I thought that if there was one person in the world I would particularly want *not* to be, it was an Egyptian soldier with Shmual after me.

Shmual explained to Danny, and Danny explained to me, that the brigade was to be issued at Ein Khussub with a large number of special six-wheel-drive trucks to replace the ordinary two-wheel-drive vehicles which were its normal equipment. The six-wheelers would help the brigade to negotiate the very difficult tracks along which it had to hurry to Mitla. All Sunday the brigade awaited its six-wheelers, as well as a lot more of the special transport needed for its operation. "This was D minus one," said Danny. And Dov said, "It was bad." He himself departed from his parachute battalion that evening and rejoined the rest of his brigade at Ein Khussub after dark.

When he got there, the situation was disconcerting. Many of his special vehicles had not arrived. He had no recovery vehicles. He was due to be across the frontier in twenty hours' time, with 120 miles to travel before he even reached it. He had nothing in which to lift either the anti-aircraft battery or the engineer platoon, which had been allotted to him; so he had to leave them behind. According to his plan, the latest possible moment at which he could leave Ein Khussub was three o'clock on the morning of Monday, October 29, D-Day, in order to cross the frontier into Sinai at four o'clock that evening.

A few more vehicles came trickling in as the hours passed; and as they arrived they were allotted to units who transferred loads onto them from their ordinary two-wheel-drive trucks. As Dov was telling me this part of the story, over glasses of tea and cakes, I wrote in the margin of my notes, "Prescription for chaos." I underlined this note when Dov told me that he then decided to set off southwestward across the Negev, taking with him those vehicles that had already arrived, and leaving the rest to catch up with his forces when they could. At the same time, he got on to Southern Command and asked them to divert as many vehicles as possible from the road to Ein Khussub, and to send them instead to join the brigade at Giraffi.

No sooner had Dov issued these new orders than he was himself called back to his air base for a few final adjustments on the plan. He was not able to rejoin his forces until noon on D-Day. By this time he had hoped to have his brigade at Suweilma on the frontier, with four hours ahead of him in which to reorganize, redistribute loads, and carry out the repair and maintenance that would be necessary after the journey along those very difficult tracks. He found his brigade, not on the frontier, but only at

An Airborne Brigade in the South

Giraffi. Here he allowed them to halt for only so long as was necessary to refuel. Then he pushed on westward, to take advantage of the four hours of daylight that were left. The business of transferring loads from ordinary vehicles to the new six-wheelers would have to wait until they got to Suweilma.

From Giraffi to Suweilma there is no road at all. There is only a pass through the hills, mostly of thick sand, along which a four-wheel-drive vehicle could be coaxed, and a two-wheel-drive vehicle can sometimes be pushed, and sometimes not. Yet somehow or other the two-wheel-drive vehicles had to be got to the frontier where, after dark, Dov could afford to halt and transfer their loads to his six-wheelers.

The new six-wheel-drive trucks and other vehicles had all arrived at Giraffi, but most of them had come without adequate spares and often without tools. In some cases it was impossible even to change a wheel, and quite a few of the vehicles continued along this appalling road (which I later viewed from the air) traveling on their rims. The way was littered with broken trucks and looked at the time—they say—as if it had been subjected to a very effective air strike. Nevertheless, the leading elements of the brigade made up time, crossed the frontier at four o'clock in the afternoon according to plan, and, a little later, saw overhead the low-flying Dakotas carrying the paratroops on their way to Mitla.

This sight was an irresistible spur to Dov. Once again he dared not stop; and once again he decided to push on across the frontier in darkness. Next stop Kuntilla! At Kuntilla he would definitely halt for maintenance and reorganization. Meanwhile he called on Southern Command for vehicle spares, tires, and tracks to be dropped by parachute during the night. The supply drop was to be made at Kuntilla. But Kuntilla had yet to be captured.

Dov's leading battalion had made good use of the last half-hour of daylight. Although there was no proper track leading to Kuntilla, the forward elements reached the place at last light. The defenses were very strong and were held by a detachment of the Desert

The airborne brigade's route to Kuntilla

Frontier Force, of approximate company strength, equipped with anti-tank guns, armed jeeps and half-tracks. The position was surrounded by two barbed-wire, double-apron fences with a continuous mine field between them.

The leading airborne battalion made a wide sweep to attack the position from the westward, coming out of the sun, just as it was sinking. There was no time to worry about mine fields. They made a head-on charge at the position, with the loss of only two half-tracks and one jeep on mines, and only one man wounded. There were no casualties from enemy fire. After a few shots from gunners and riflemen dazzled by the sunset, the Egyptians abandoned their defenses, scrambled through their own wire, and, as night fell on D-Day, disappeared barefoot into the dusk. Nobody wanted to stop them.

The main trouble, at this stage, was not the enemy, but the lack of spare parts for the vehicles. A half-track which ran into an anti-personnel mine and blew a tire had to carry on with a flat tire, 40 miles as the crow flies, 60 as the track takes you, to Nakhl. As Dov said, "The convoy had been torn to pieces by the heavy going." Apart from the multitude of wheeled vehicles that was now littering the way behind, half the light tanks had become immobilized. Out of eighteen field guns, only one had reached Kuntilla. The petrol lorries were stuck somewhere toward the rear of the column, unable to get past the disabled vehicles. As more and more vehicles went out of action, those that remained had to carry increased loads which, in consequence, made them still more prone to collapse under the strain of the route.

Reluctantly Dov had to order a halt and to sacrifice time for the sake of some measure of reorganization. During the night petrol and spare parts, as well as tires, were dropped by parachute. A Piper Cub landed in the darkness and took away the wounded man as well as a letter to Southern Command explaining the urgent need for further supplies to be dropped by air along the route.

Within five hours of taking Kuntilla, Dov's leading battalion was in good enough shape to continue the advance. It was desperately urgent to take the very strong position at Thamed; and if this could not be done under cover of darkness, it might be a very tough proposition by daylight. At ten o'clock that evening, D-Day, the leading battalion moved forward, followed an hour later by brigade headquarters. A force was left behind at Kuntilla to collect stragglers and bring them along later.

The distance from Kuntilla to Thamed is 40 miles as the track runs, and the track is not good. It was not until four o'clock in the morning that the advance guard reached Thamed. Thamed itself, which is an important watering point, is not defensible and was not defended. The Thamed positions were sited on precipitous cliffs, five miles farther west. There is a road junction here, and the defenses were constructed around it. They were held by two infantry companies detached from a battalion of the Desert Frontier Force which was stationed at Nakhl. The road passed through the middle of the defensive perimeter of the Thamed positions; and since the positions could not be bypassed, they had to be taken before Dov could continue his advance toward Mitla. He decided to do so at dawn. He went in from the east, and again he had the sun behind him—this time at the moment of sunrise.

His plan was extremely simple. It had to be. Apart from the desperate need for speed, there was no way of getting up the steep and often precipitous slopes except by the main road which ran slap through the middle of the perimeter. On each side of the main road there were formidable mine fields enclosed within barbed-wire fences.

The battalion commander deployed two infantry companies in half-tracks astride the main road. Behind them came the rest of his battalion, also deployed, with strict orders to keep moving. They were in open six-wheelers. The whole battalion then charged straight toward the Egyptian position. Even to the Egyptians it must have seemed a gift, straight from Balaklava, when they opened fire with five machine guns from the top of the cliffs.

But this ridiculous charge continued merrily. At the last moment, the leading half-track swerved onto the road and, with the others following, drove straight through the main gate into the Egyptian positions. It was blown up by a mine, and the company commander was wounded. But he ordered his company to push on past him, and he covered their advance with smoke grenades thrown from his wrecked half-track. The rest of the battalion followed.

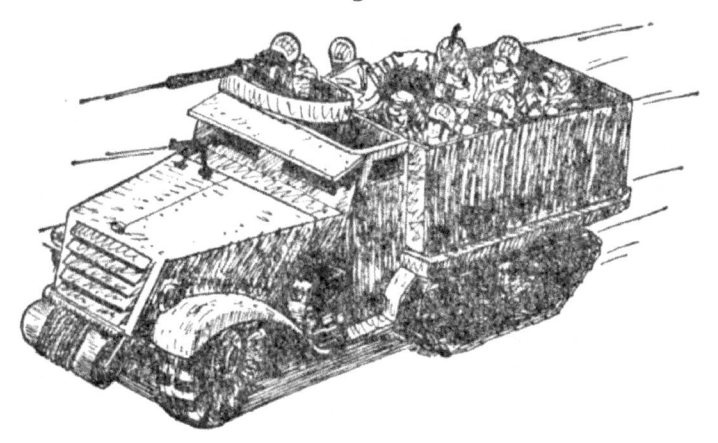

The ridiculous charge

The Thamed positions, held by a couple of companies, would, by any military standards, be rated impregnable against anything less than a full brigade attacking with artillery support under cover of darkness. Yet the moment they were penetrated by Dov's half-tracks, their defenders ceased opposition. Again, as at Kuntilla, they took to their bare feet, leaving 60 dead behind them. Dov lost 3 killed and 6 wounded.

Thamed was taken by six o'clock in the morning, and by eight o'clock the airborne troops were attacked by a pair of MIG fighters and suffered casualties.

The brigade commander was now faced with something of a problem. By eleven o'clock in the morning a substantial part of his convoy had collected and reorganized itself and had been supplied with spare parts from the air. The question was whether to push on in daylight despite the air attacks, which might be expected to increase, or to remain dispersed until nightfall. A Piper Cub was sent to the Mitla area for information and returned with a message from the forward battalion saying that it had been subjected to several air attacks, in which a Piper Cub had been destroyed; that it had a number of wounded; that it had begun to receive heavy fire from mortars and was trying to silence them with its own mortars; that it intended to attack in the evening but was expecting in the meanwhile to be attacked itself. It asked urgently for air support.

According to the self-imposed ordinances of the Israel Air Force, these attacks by Egyptian aircraft permitted the opening of air hostilities. The brigade commander was told by General Headquarters that from one o'clock that afternoon he could ask for air support. He requested it immediately on the Mitla area and decided himself to push on, along the 40 miles to Nakhl, as quickly as possible. He advanced with his vehicles dispersed at wide intervals to avoid casualties from the air, but enemy aircraft ceased to operate against him as soon as Israel's fighters appeared in support.

Proposing to attack Nakhl at last light, he asked for air support at four o'clock that afternoon. But one of the aircraft returning from Mitla sent him a message to say that there were many vehicles moving eastward from the canal toward the passes. Therefore Dov asked that the air strike on Nakhl should be diverted to these vehicles. And at a quarter to five that afternoon he attacked Nakhl, with three companies on half-tracks. It was an important supply base for the whole area and was held by a battalion (less the two companies which had been at Thamed). By half past five, the place was taken by the Israelis with no casualties. The Egyptians who were holding this fairly formidable position lost 10 men killed and 25 taken prisoner. The remainder ran into the desert.

Dov had intended that the leading battalion should stop at Nakhl, a most important junction of roads leading north to Bir Hasana and the main central axis to Ismailia, and also northeastward to Kuseima, Sabha, and the Israel frontier at El Auja. But he dared not waste time. Accordingly he told this battalion to push straight on and make contact with his parachute forces in the Mitla area; and the second battalion, which was still several hours behind, would hold Nakhl when it got there. By this rearrangement Dov saved several precious hours and was able to join his paratroops by ten o'clock that night (D plus 1).

Meanwhile, despite the air situation, and contrary to orders, a number of Piper Cubs had landed along the route to evacuate the wounded. Before Dov left Nakhl at six o'clock that evening, he got news that all his wounded men were safely in hospital at Elath.

The parachute battalion was to be dropped in the eastern mouth of the Mitla Passes at what is known as the "Monument." This is a plinth erected on a small knoll to the memory of Colonel A. C. Palmer, D.S.O., a British officer who was twice governor of Sinai and who won great renown amongst the nomadic Arabs of Transjordan, Hedjaz, and Sinai. At the Monument the parachute battalion would form up and establish itself in the eastern part of the Mitla Passes. Here it would await the arrival of the rest of the brigade before advancing farther toward the canal.

The Mitla Passes are very narrow and some twenty miles in length. For most of the way the road is encased by steep, often precipitous, hills which are of sheer rock perforated by deep fissures and caves that offer the most perfect emplacements for machine guns and other weapons with excellent fields of fire up and down the route. They are safe against anything except a direct hit; and they can be assaulted only on foot—a foot that has to be shod and practiced for a scramble, and sometimes a technical climb, up difficult rock. The question was: Could the Israeli paratroops secure these positions before the Egyptian reinforcements reached them? There was another question that was even more pressing: What were the chances that Israel's Dakotas could get to the Mitla area, and drop their battalion, without being shot down by Egyptian fighters?

A senior officer of Israel's Air Force told me, "There was scarcely a principle of war applicable to this type of operation which did not have to be jettisoned. You just don't drop a battalion in an area forty miles from an enemy fighter airfield and a hundred and eighty miles from your own. We couldn't do it by night, for fear of not finding the right place. You just don't do that sort of thing by daylight; and if you must, then your only hope is to knock hell out of the enemy airfield before you start." This was something that Israel was prohibited from doing. According to the stringent rules of the game—the "Yalu River rule"—Israeli aircraft could neither cross the canal nor attack any enemy aircraft until the latter had attacked first.

"The plan was just nuts," said the commander of the wing concerned, "but we did the best we could. We kept a patrol of Mystères 'continuously' at ten thousand feet over the east bank of the canal from the time the Dakotas came within radar range to the time they had dropped their troops and had turned homeward." For the sake of other laymen like myself, I should explain that the word "continuously" has, in this case, a technical significance meaning that the patrols would have to be relieved periodically, since each could remain over the area for only a few minutes. They were operating at extreme range from their base.

"We flew the Dakotas at very low altitude," the wing commander said, "to give them a chance of escaping radar detection. As a matter of fact, with their camouflage they were very difficult to detect visually from above. Even their own fighter escorts lost sight of them on occasions!"

The escort was composed of Ouragans and Meteors, several of each "continuously," to accompany the Dakotas in layers of pairs flying at different altitudes. Since all these aircraft fly at different speeds—the Meteors being of course much faster than the Dakotas, and the Ouragans much faster than the Meteors—the pairs of aircraft at their particular altitudes had to fly on a crisscross course so as to keep formation with each other, as well as to keep company with the Dakotas; and since the Dakotas themselves were flying in separate sections, the planning and timing of this escort presented a nice problem of staff work.

Yet the main air problem was not the initial drop but the maintenance all night of an aerial railway for bringing supplies by the same aircraft. They flew sortie after sortie, keeping up a continuous stream all that night from dusk to dawn, and on the three nights that followed. It was a tremendous strain not only on the air crews, but also on the ground staffs who had to refuel and reload aircraft between their sorties. All international records were broken during the next few nights, although many of the ground staff, as well as a few of the air crew, were reservists who had been called up only 48 hours before operations started.

So far as the drop was concerned, there has never yet been an airborne operation, by any army and air force, in which the air crews and the troops have been agreed about the accuracy of their position. And despite the fact that the Israeli air crews and paratroops have a particularly close relationship—many of the former have chosen to undergo parachute training, so that they wear the silver parachute on an airman's blue tunic—they are no exception to the standing rule of post-operational disagreement. The Air Force says that it dropped the paratroops precisely as planned; the paratroops say that when they hit the desert they were five miles too far to the east.

The drop of the battalion was otherwise made without incident, in good order, and with only 13 men injured, 2 of whom had broken legs, and the rest sprained ankles. The force advanced rapidly westward in the direction of the Monument. In the darkness it came to a small hill, which is too low to be marked on the map and which was assumed to be the beginning of the hills that enclose the Monument. In fact it was a mile short of the mouth of the pass.

At this point there is a road junction, or fork, and it was here that the paratroop battalion established its perimeter on ground which seemed to offer good defensive positions, but which was, in fact, rather too small for a whole battalion. During that night, and for most of the next day, the men dug themselves in. It was hard work, because the ground was stony.

Patrols had been sent forward to the entrance of the pass, and ambushes were set on the two roads leading from the fork. During the day they attacked Egyptian transports, killing some 40 Egyptians, and captured a most valuable prize—a lorry carrying drums of water. Water was short, even though at midnight on D-Day there had been a supply drop in which water had been included. A battery of 120-mm. mortars had also been dropped on the perimeter; and by dawn on D plus 1, the paratroop battalion had established an airstrip.

At noon that day, the first Egyptian attack, of approximately two platoons supported by mortars, was launched from the direction of the Monument. A company from the paratroop battalion was sent out to meet it and to destroy the enemy mortars, but was recalled when Israeli jet planes appeared in support. The Israeli aircraft destroyed the mortars, and the advancing infantry were dispersed by fire from the paratroops' own mortars which had been dropped during the night.

During that afternoon of D plus 1, the Israel Air Force reported to the paratroop battalion that numbers of the enemy were disorganized and retreating westward and that many enemy vehicles had been destroyed. The attacks by the Israel Air Force continued until dark. The night was quiet, interrupted only by the arrival of Dov and his leading battalion a little after ten o'clock.

When Dov reached his parachute battalion in the middle of the night, he was faced with something of a problem. The pimple on which they were entrenched, and which covered their airstrip, was not large enough for the deployment of his whole brigade. The air attacks which this battalion had already experienced would probably be intensified the next morning. There was also news of Egyptian armor not far away to the north; and the pimple was surrounded by level ground only too suitable for tank warfare. In the circumstances it was not a good defensive position; but there was no alternative except to advance westward into the hills of the Mitla Passes, and these were now held by two Egyptian battalions which had crossed the canal the previous afternoon. Accordingly, Dov got orders from General Headquarters that, for the time being, he was to remain where he was. Dov had to make the best of it.

A few hours before dawn the whole of his brigade was concentrating in this area. To meet the possibility of attack by both air and armor, he dispersed his vehicles and ordered one battalion to dig in with the utmost urgency. The other battalion was sent back about four miles to take up positions in a wadi where the ground was more broken and provided some sort of cover. The artillery was brought forward and dug itself into positions facing west.

At a quarter to six in the morning, the brigade was attacked by four Egyptian Vampires, but almost immediately these were met by two Ouragans, which shot down all the enemy aircraft. At half past eleven, the second-in-command of Southern Command flew in by Piper Cub and gave permission for the brigade to go forward cautiously, but without committing itself to any large-scale attack.

Dov started his advance with two companies early in the afternoon. Almost immediately they were involved in very heavy fighting. The Egyptians were established in caves and fissures of the rock whence they completely commanded the passes. Dov's leading troops were pinned down, and he reinforced them with another company which climbed to the top of the hills on the northern wall of the pass and attempted to attack downward. It met very heavy fire from the opposite hillside and was soon involved in the same kind of hand-to-hand fighting which the Americans had found so costly against the Japanese in similar situations. At one moment the Egyptians tried to escape from their caves; but when they found this impossible, they continued the battle with courage.

Late in the afternoon an attack was made by Egyptian Meteors escorted by six MIGs. The MIGs were met by two Israel Mystères, but the Meteors succeeded in blowing up an ammunition wagon and inflicting severe casualties. Despite the continuous fire from land and air, over 60 Israel casualties were evacuated by half-tracks during that afternoon and carried out of danger.

Shortly before dark, Dov had a company established in the hills on each side of the road. With bazookas and grenades they cleared both positions after three hours of heavy fighting in the darkness.

An Airborne Brigade in the South

Meanwhile, the brigade was running short of supplies. It lit the airstrip and shortly afterward received a supply drop from Dakotas. These aircraft had been ordered not to land, because the airstrip was considered inadequate. But when they were told of the numbers of wounded waiting to be evacuated, no less than 12 of them came down and took away 120 wounded before midnight. There were also nearly 40 dead.

At midnight the position still seemed critical. The Mitla Passes had yet to be taken, and the threat remained of enemy armor in the north. Dov had to redisperse his forces. He started to give out orders to his battalion commanders, whom he had assembled at his headquarters. They were usually an argumentative lot, but on this occasion they remained remarkably silent. "Any questions?" Dov asked. There were none. There was no answer. All the battalion commanders were asleep, and Dov was falling asleep himself. Nobody had had any sleep for the past three nights. Dov then made his wisest decision; he told everyone to rest.

Toward morning, Dov woke his unit commanders and reorganized his forces. By dawn everybody was dug in within a defensive perimeter, including all the oddments of the force and the airstrip detachments. By then he had organized a mobile reserve consisting of those tanks which had been recovered and made serviceable, and every half-track that could still move. This reserve force was sent away to a flank and hidden in a wadi. By daybreak Dov felt himself ready for anything, from any direction whether armored or not. Nothing came.

A Piper Cub made a reconnaissance and reported that there was no enemy armor in the neighborhood. Patrols were sent out into the Mitla Passes, where they mopped up a few nearby positions. Then Dov advanced westward and took the farther passes, from which the Egyptians had gone in the night, and got to the coastal road which was his objective. Later, a force was sent south along this road to help with the capture of Sharm El Sheikh. In the event, its help was not needed, and the place was taken without it.

Paratrooper at Mitla

All this was told to me by Dov and his merry men during a most pleasant day that I spent with them at their headquarters. They gave me a wonderful lunch. When it was over, we all sat on low stools around a table where Turkish coffee was served to us and Dov said, "Now, Colonel, tell us something about the British Commandos." He wanted details of some of the raids I had taken part in, and of the many others I had helped to plan at Combined Operations Headquarters. I tried to comply with his request. I did not get very far with any of my stories before one or other of the officers was correcting me on points of detail. These boys study the details of battles with fervor. They knew more about many of the operations that I had planned than I did myself.

A few days later I flew in a Piper Cub along the route taken by that brigade. I spent an airsick half-hour going round and round the scene of the Mitla fighting. On each circuit that we made, I was able to detect yet more and more of those enemy positions hidden in the caves.

I have tried to imagine myself into the circumstances of those troops, after their six days of traveling, their three sleepless nights, and their day of very heavy fighting. I can only say that Dov's actions during that last night—the redeployment of his forces and their reorganization for the attack that he expected at dawn—must have needed a lot of will power, apart from military competence and physical endurance.

"We were in fact a bit tired," said Shmual from his chair. He climbed out of it wearily and shambled off to look for some more cigarettes. I gave him a light for his cigarette, but hesitantly and very cautiously, for fear I should set fire to his beard and start a general conflagration. Dov was watching intently; I had a feeling that he hoped this might happen.

VI

The Improbable Route

THE Sinai mountains of the deep south have a painful kind of beauty; it hurts; it provokes emotions from a source deeper than is often tapped. Beautiful in a lunar way; theatrically splendid, of course, at sunrise across the Gulf of Aqaba and at sunset across the Gulf of Suez; but, above all, decisively beautiful for their significance. Wasn't it here that a scruffy parcel of escaped slaves, desolately wandering through a wilderness which is unbelievably wild—and knowing what they were running away *from,* but with no notion of what they were running away *to*—was given the Law of God from out of the thunder and lightning, from out of the still, small voice, of this mountain below me?

Below me? It seemed a gross impertinence that the pilot and I should be tossing about like capricious bugs in a little Piper Cub above the Mountain of God. It was also uncomfortable.

There is very little room in a Piper Cub for a passenger with long legs. At 10,800 feet, with the peaks not far below us, it was bitterly cold. A quarter of an hour earlier, it had been sweating hot on the airfield. Now I had cramp in one thigh and a pain in my stomach from starting too early in the morning without breakfast. I was shivering down my spine and feeling slightly sick from the eddies that threw us about like a casual joke. But this was Mount Sinai, and below it the Monastery of St. Catherine, which is nearly 1500 years old and has no entrance, they say, except by way of a cradle which the monks haul up to their ramparts on ropes.

There are trees all up the valley, and round the corner in a hairpin bend, by the monastery. And there are half a dozen other houses with green around them, seen from the air. Green! In all these mountains belonging to the southern third of the Sinai Peninsula—the triangle that you get by chopping off the tip from Elath on the east to Abu Rudeis on the west—there is nothing green at all, except just here.

I had been warned to look out for the Malachite Mountains which, when the sun strikes them, shine with bewildering loveliness. I failed to find them. Indeed, except for a few moments at sunrise and again at sunset, these moon-mountains, with their precipitous slopes and wadis, could be painted in oils with nothing on the palette but black and white and raw and burnt sienna. There is nothing more blue than you can get with a mixture of black and white; nothing more green than from raw sienna and black; nothing more yellow than from raw sienna and white; nothing more red or crimson or purple than comes from burnt sienna mixed in various proportions with the rest. The dominant color is a deep dull red.

These mountains do not need vivid colors. Their beauty is more intense because it owes nothing to color; because it subdues you despite its lack of color, despite its monotony, and only on account of significance and shape.

They are very strange shapes. Sometimes a great spiked fang is thrust up at your airplane. Sometimes there is an entirely flat tableland of about a square mile, dead level on the top of 8000 feet. And sometimes the walls are carved into the twisted pillars of a temple, or hewn into forms coming straight from a forgotten dress with no likeness whatever to anything that is in the heavens above, or on the earth beneath, or in the waters under the earth.

I apologize! This is a political and military account of the Sinai Campaign. But by way of apology, I can only assert that there is not an Israel soldier, whether a recent immigrant or a third-generation Sabra gathered in from any one of the sixty nations, who would not have shared my feelings—but in his own way, certainly in his own way peculiar to himself, at the sight of Mount Sinai, the beginnings of Judaism, Christianity, and the Moslem faith, the well of truth on the top of a mountain, the spring of human strength in a small, still voice. And if I really hoped to describe the Israeli—a thing that I have been trying to do obliquely ever since I started this book—I should struggle to explain more cleverly the effect of these mountains on a human heart.

I am supposed to be describing the operations of the 9th Brigade which (in Phase III of the plan) was to move down the coast of the Gulf of Aqaba and take Sharm el Sheikh. Through the eastern outposts of these red mountains, the way of the brigade had led them from Ras El Naqb, northwest of Elath, down through 200 miles of obstruction to the southern tip of the peninsula. In many places the road seems from the air to be nothing better than a mule track running through steep, sometimes precipitous, passes. Except at Nuweiba, and again at Dahab, it does not approach the sea until it comes out in the broad space of sand with only a few pimples of red rock at Ras Nasrani where the major defenses of the Egyptians had been sited. From here, for 12 miles to the southwest, this sandy plain runs, with a wall of mountains on one side and the sea on the other, to the military township, harbor, and wide bay of Sharm el Sheikh.

Ras Nasrani and Sharm el Sheikh had once been Arab hamlets; but their inhabitants were removed by the Egyptians in 1952 when Egypt decided on the costly but effective project of injuring Israel economically by closing the Gulf of Aqaba and the port of Elath to her seaborne trade. Ras Nasrani and Sharm el Sheikh were nothing but coastal redoubts, designed solely to close the narrow passage into the gulf, between the islet of Tiran and the mainland. They had cost many millions of dollars to construct, and as many more to maintain. Their permanent garrisons amounted to 2100 men.

Two sizable ships supplied them permanently with fuel, food, and water—for it is an almost waterless place. In addition, there were purifying plants for making fresh water from salt water.

To augment her seaborne supplies to these bases, Egypt had built about 80 miles of new road, an extension of the route which already ran down the eastern coast of the Gulf of Suez, through a few oil wells and a manganese mine, to El Tor. As has already been told, this road could be reached from Israel, across the Sinai Peninsula, by way of Mitla. The military possibilities were obvious. While the 9th Brigade was finding an improbable route down the east coast of the peninsula to Sharm el Sheikh, the airborne brigade, once it had forced the Mitla Passes, could drive there from the west. These two forces would converge upon the Egyptian fortifications from both directions, and, if necessary, make a coordinated assault. I had better repeat that, in fact, the 9th Brigade took its objectives without the actual intervention of the force from Mitla.

The islet of Tiran lies in the entrance to the Gulf of Aqaba about two miles east of Ras Nasrani. The Egyptians had scarcely fortified this island. There was no need to do so. Owing to the coral reefs and other navigational hazards, there is only a narrow channel to the west of Tiran, between it and Ras Nasrani, through which ships can pass into the Gulf of Aqaba to the port of Elath. Here they had to run directly under the six-inch and three-inch naval guns which the Egyptians had put at Ras Nasrani. These batteries completely controlled the only sea lane into the gulf and they had closed it effectively for the past four years.

On the night of October 26, when the 9th Brigade was first ordered to mobilize, it was up somewhere in the northern area which is its home. It is a reserve brigade, and its men are mostly farmers rather than townsfolk. Many of them have a high degree of mechanical aptitude, and most of them are tough, even by Israeli standards. Within forty-eight hours their mobilization was completed and they had been equipped and made mobile with their normal complement of vehicles, mostly civilian. Many of the vehicles were later to be replaced, like those of the airborne division, by special six-wheelers which would be more suitable—if any wheeled vehicles were in any way suitable—for the route they were to take.

During the night of October 28, the brigade started its movement south to their assembly area. This preliminary move was to be a matter of 200 miles, and, owing to the congested state of the roads during the hours of darkness, it could not be completed in a single night. During the day of October 29 (D-Day), the vehicles of the brigade continued to infiltrate in small numbers southward into the Negev. On D plus 1, the special six-wheelers arrived, and the two-wheel-drive vehicles which they were to replace were sent back. At five o'clock in the morning of October 31 (D plus 2), the brigade was 20 miles south of Beersheba on the route which leads southward across the frontier through Giraffi to Kuntilla.

I have already described this route, which had been taken two days previously by the airborne brigade. It had been bad enough for them, but their passage had made it far more difficult for those who had to follow. For seventeen hours, the 9th Brigade coaxed its vehicles through the 70 miles of thick sand to Kuntilla, which it reached at ten o'clock that night. It was then in enemy territory, although there was no enemy about. Throughout the night it continued southward for another thirty miles or so to its final assembly area at Ras el Naqb. Here it was ordered to delay its departure for twenty-four hours.

This delay, which was accepted impatiently by the 9th Brigade, was a great boon. During that day and night men could rest, and the vehicles could be repaired after the ardors of the route behind them in readiness for the far greater ardors of the road ahead. For once, in an Israeli campaign, there was a little time in hand in which a force could organize and prepare itself. The time was well spent.

All military commanders are, of necessity, individualists. If they were not, then they would not, or should not, be commanding any

"Avraham," commander of the 9th Brigade

sizable body of troops. But the Israeli commanders are more individualistic than any others that one is ever likely to meet; and the commander of the 9th Brigade is even more individualistic than most of his colleagues. He is a big, burly man, full of fun, forceful and thoughtful. Any soldier would say that this was the sort of man he would like to have as his commander in a strenuous and hazardous expedition. His first name is Avraham. During the early part of 1956 he attended the Senior Officers' School in Britain. By my hand he sends greetings to his fellow students.

It was with intent that I used the words "strenuous" and "hazardous" about this expedition. It was likely to be both and in that order. First, there was the difficult drive to the assembly area. Next the approach through enemy territory, along those 200 miles of rocky track alternating with deep sand, up and down steep hills and through precipitous passes. And at the end of it there was to be an assault on positions that were more strongly prepared than any others in the whole peninsula.

Everything depended, of course, on getting the brigade to the battle without substantial casualties to its vehicles from the rigors of the route. To accomplish this, which itself was a major military feat, Avraham took certain measures which may be compared or contrasted with those of the airborne brigade traveling to Mitla by difficult but much less arduous tracks. This must not be taken as criticism against the airborne brigade. As I explained in the last chapter, that force had had no time in which to organize itself or to prepare for an orderly advance. Its primary and exclusive concern had been to get cracking westward to reinforce the battalion that had been dropped by parachute. It had had little choice but to pile men, weapons, equipment, and stores onto any vehicle that could still move and, when it refused to move any farther, to transfer its load onto something else.

By contrast, the 9th Brigade had time to organize itself deliberately. It was to move in four forces or detachments. Force A, comprising a reconnaissance company with 3-inch mortars, and an infantry company in half-tracks with 120-mm. mortars, would lead the way and be ready to fight. It was followed by a temporary force (A.1) consisting of three platoons drawn from the rearmost battalion. These platoons were to provide flank guards to block tracks which led into the main route while the column was passing. When the rest of the column had gone by, each platoon in turn would rejoin its own battalion at the tail of the column. Following this temporary force came forward brigade headquarters and its air tentacle.

Next came Force B, consisting of one battalion with heavy mortars. This battalion was only two companies strong, since it had already provided the company in half-tracks which was part of

Force A. It was followed by rear brigade headquarters and Force C, consisting of the last battalion, from which the flank guards had been detached. This force also contained the main body of the workshop, medical, and other units, and a battalion of field guns, twenty-five-pounders. Speaking as a gunner, I will say now (and hereafter hold my peace) that these guns were never able to open fire during the whole operation. But at least they left their limbers behind them—which is more than can be said of those with the airborne brigade; otherwise they would never have covered the course.

The total number of vehicles accompanying this brigade was 220. Nearly half of them had civilian drivers, over age and strangers to the brigade. Yet all but 10 vehicles arrived in good order, and in their proper place, at Sharm el Sheikh. I do not know how to describe the magnitude of this feat to anyone who has not taken a brigade on wheels and tracks along a route such as this—and, apart from Avraham, I do not know of anyone who has ever done so. Speaking, for the moment, as a soldier to other soldiers, I can only say that the task is out of the question.

To make it even more questionable, Avraham laid it down that no vehicle should carry more than 2½ tons. In every case this load had to include gasoline, oil, and water for five days. Throughout the column there were dispersed three detachments (or LADs) of the main workshop, one for each of the sub-forces. When a vehicle broke down, it was bustled off the route and the LAD started to work on it. If the LAD was unable to get it mobile again by the time the tail of the sub-force had passed, the vehicle was left to the main workshop. When, in due course, the workshop came up, it was told by the driver what mechanical first aid had already been given and it started from that point on whatever major repairs were necessary. The 10 vehicles from the whole force that were damaged beyond repair were stripped to pieces by the main workshop and turned into spares for the rest.

Quite apart from the mechanical difficulties of the course, there was the human element. Nobody had more than a few hours' sleep

The improbable route

during the two days of the march; and everybody was frequently engaged in pushing, hauling, and coaxing his truck over, or round, or through this ridiculous obstacle course. And at the end of it he had to be ready to fight. One of the reasons given by Avraham for the excellent order in which his force arrived at the site of what might have been, and ought to have been, a very bloody battle, was the fact that the average age of his men was somewhere between 30 and 35, much higher than for most of the Israel Army. Men in their twenties are the speediest on foot, but those in their thirties have greater endurance.

The force left its assembly area at Ras el Naqb at five o'clock on the morning of D plus 4. Although the going was difficult from the start, there were no major hitches until noon that day. By this time, they had reached Ein el Furtaga, about 10 miles inland from the Gulf of Aqaba, northeast of Nuweiba. The next 10 miles ran between boulders, along a track which allowed only a few inches on either side of a vehicle. The way was uphill and steep and the going was in deep sand. Every single-wheel vehicle had to be pushed and hauled up it by hand. This was done in about six hours, by nightfall.

The way immediately ahead was equally difficult, but it lay downhill, so that the hauling and shoving would be much less laborious. Before continuing, the brigade rested and fed itself and did not set off again until four o'clock the next morning, D plus 5, an hour before first light. The next 30 miles were covered in ten hours and the head of the brigade reached Dahab at three o'clock that afternoon. Here it rested for two full hours, for refueling and maintenance, leaving again at nightfall, and traveling another 30 miles before it made contact with the enemy at daylight on the following morning, D plus 6.

At Dahab there was a small Arab village, long deserted, and a prepared defensive position. But this had been abandoned by the Egyptians before the brigade reached them. Here there is also a suitable place for beaching landing craft; and two of these craft (LCMs) brought a load of gasoline and an AMX light tank. (I must leave until a little later the story of how these craft got into the Gulf of Aqaba.)

On the stretch running southward from Dahab to a bend in the track about 10 miles northwest of Naqb, there were some of the most difficult obstacles of the whole route. It was not surprising that when the head of the column at last made contact with enemy elements it halted to discover the strength of the opposition. Nobody but its commander would censure it for not pushing ahead at daybreak, and for wasting the best part of an hour before discovering that the ambush, which consisted of a specially picked officer and 20 selected "crack troops," was not prepared to do more than let off a few shots.

The commander, Avraham, was perhaps made hypercritical by a weird experience that had fallen upon him during the previous night. At one stage he had called a halt for a few hours' sleep.

"Avraham, Avraham—where are you?"

Thirty miles to the westward, Mount Sinai stood in the night. As the commander lay down to rest, the radio receiver of his air tentacle was beside him. Suddenly a voice came out of it, out of the darkness, out of Mount Sinai: "Avraham, Avraham—where are you?"

The brigade commander answered, "Avraham is here."

The voice spoke again, "I am the father of Yael and the husband of Ruth. Do you know me?"

Avraham answered, "I know the voice."

The voice asked, "How are your flocks?"

"The flocks are fine."

"Fine?"

"Yes, fine."

"And how are your camels?" the voice asked.

"Okay," Avraham answered.

"Okay?"

"Okay," Avraham repeated.

"Then drive faster!" said the voice and was silent.

The Improbable Route

The name of General Dayan's daughter is Yael, and his wife is Ruth. In the War of Independence the words "flocks" and "camels" were used as code names for "troops" and "vehicles," respectively.

After the ambush—the first contact with the enemy—the brigade left the mountains and reached the coastal strip at Naqb. There was no enemy here. Five miles to the south lay the fortification of Ras Nasrani, and the naval batteries. These defenses were built around the guns. They consisted of fence after fence of barbed wire, with mine fields between them. The barbed wire is so thick that, seen from the ground, it resembles a forest, blocking the view of the inevitable mirage beyond it. Within the barbed wire there were concrete machine-gun positions, gun emplacements, and deep bunkers, all interconnected by a network of trenches. And all deserted.

The cost of these defenses would have nourished a few thousand fellaheen for a good many years, but the Egyptian commander had abandoned them on getting the report that "a reconnaissance detachment consisting of several tracked vehicles was moving south and would fall upon him in about six days' time." At this alarming news he withdrew his 1500 men within the perimeter of the position at Sharm el Sheikh, where all his supplies were dumped. The Sharm el Sheikh defenses were not nearly as strong as those that he had abandoned. Neither had he the room or the time to get so many men deployed there, and dug in, to tactical advantage.

This Egyptian commander was something of a character. He was a very nice man, so his captors insist. When Nasser had ordered him to withdraw, he refused to do so but declared his desire to stand and fight. He came directly under command of General Headquarters in Cairo, and his forces comprised a full-scale infantry battalion, a National Guard battalion, 2 six-inch and 4 three-inch naval guns, 6 six-pounder anti-tank guns, plenty of mortars, both three-inch and 4.2, and nearly 40 Bren carriers.

Before stripping himself for action, so to speak, the Egyptian commander had dispatched two steamers carrying the sick and the weak—anyone, as he put it, "who would hamper my fighting ability." He was supplied with 200 cubic meters of water, as well as a purification plant sufficient to water his troops from the sea for an indefinite period. He had food for several months, including 500 live sheep. His 1500 men who remained after the purge of some 600 sick and weak were commanded by 43 officers, including one full colonel, two lieutenant colonels, and ten majors, all of whom were in due course put into the bag. The full colonel was the area commander. The man in charge of the battle was the commander of the regular infantry battalion. His name was Neguib, but he claimed no connection with the other one.

Lieutenant Colonel Khana Neguib gave three reasons for the defeat of his force of 1500 men, all strongly entrenched, by a force of equal size. First, his morale was shattered by the air attacks which had been made by a few Mustangs and still fewer B-17s during the previous days. (They had inflicted a minute number of actual casualties.) Second, he had no artillery support. And his third reason, as has been mentioned earlier, was that his men were no good.

When asked why he had abandoned the Ras Nasrani positions —despite his warlike protestation to Nasser that he intended to hold them to the last—Neguib explained that his military textbooks directed that a force should be kept concentrated. He had chosen to concentrate in Sharm El Sheikh.

Neguib did not surrender Sharm el Sheikh without a fight. He must be given credit for ordering his naval detachments to spike their guns before withdrawing from Ras Nasrani, and for actually seeing that they did so. Moreover, when they had withdrawn to Sharm el Sheikh, they inflicted casualties on the 9th Brigade before capitulation. The brigade had 10 men killed and 33 wounded.

The brigade made contact with the Sharm el Sheikh defenses at four o'clock in the afternoon of D plus 6. Many of these defenses were very well prepared and truly strong. Their right flank was on the sea, and their left rested on a ridge running parallel with the

"Point three—my men were no good."

coast. It was along this ridge that Avraham decided to attack with six companies under cover of darkness. The attack was led by infantry in half-tracks and was launched at three-thirty in the morning. In places there was tough fighting, since the Egyptians had no hope of escape and nowhere to run away to. Many of the emplacements had to be reduced by hand grenades, and it was six hours before the garrison surrendered, at nine-thirty, after the loss of about 200 men killed.

Avraham is a stickler for the Geneva Convention. Therefore he fed his captives on Israeli rations and fed his own troops on the excellent Egyptian supplies, including the 500 live sheep.

So far I have only hinted that this was, to some extent, a combined operation. Five medium-sized landing craft (LCMs) were taken from Haifa to the port of Elath, and were ready to support the brigade during its move south, to supply it with fuel and anything else that it might need, and to bring it light tanks.

This was not exclusively a naval occasion, since the landing craft were taken overland, a distance of 220 miles as the crow flies. This was not easy. An LCM weighs nearly 30 tons and is about 14 feet wide. It can carry a light tank.

The decision to get them to Elath was taken at midnight on the 26th of October. It was scarcely a feasible proposition, but the breaking of the blockade in the Gulf of Aqaba had been a long-term naval ambition and the Navy was desperately keen to have some part in it.

The original plan had been to carry the landing craft on tank transporters; but to do this would have meant the risk of blocking the only two roads to the south, both of which were already gravely congested. Accordingly, the Navy was forbidden to use tank transporters and for a few sad hours it seemed that the project would have to be abandoned. It was six hours, in fact. By the end of that time, experiments had been made, and the naval engineers had discovered that railway trucks could be modified or adapted to carry landing craft as far as Beersheba. From there onward, the craft would fit on to the special auto-cars which were normally used for transporting phosphates from the Dead Sea to Haifa. That these auto-cars had had to be purchased solely because the port of Elath could not be used for exporting the Dead Sea phosphates provided a pleasant pinch of spice to this land-borne naval project.

It was not very easy to modify the railway trucks for this purpose. But between midnight on the 27th and midday on the 28th, the Navy and the railway officials between them designed and constructed a special cradle. At noon loading began. This was itself an engineering problem, and it was not until eight o'clock that night that the train was ready to start. It was then found that a house on the outskirts of Haifa was a little too close to the railway line to allow the trucks to pass. They moved the railway line ten inches away from it, to clear the house. They sent ahead a dummy mock-up which gave them warning that several railway signals and other devices, including a passenger bridge at one station, had to be removed to allow the train to pass. It reached Beersheba at dawn on D-Day.

It took all day to lift the landing craft from the train and get them on the auto-cars. It took two further days to drive them down from Beersheba to Elath. They were, of course, heavily camouflaged; but they could only move by night, since, in many places, they were less than a mile from the Jordan frontier. And when they reached Elath, which is just across the way from the port of Aqaba, arrangements had to be made that would ensure the launching of the craft without the Jordan observation posts' discovering what was up.

By daylight on D plus 3—while the 9th Brigade was waiting at Nabq—the 5 LCMs were seaborne. At three o'clock that afternoon, 2 LCMs, each armed with 2 machine guns, "bombarded" Taba, just across the frontier, where there was a small Egyptian detachment which ran away. Simultaneously, another LCM loaded with petrol started to sail the 63 miles down to Dahab, where it met the 9th Brigade and unloaded the supplies on the beach, during the course of D plus 4.

On D plus 5, a combined operation was undertaken against the island of Tiran. After a brisk bombardment from the LCMs' machine guns, a platoon was landed there, only to find that the detachment manning the place had already swum to the mainland to be put into the bag at Sharm el Sheikh.

At Elath there had already been an armed trawler, and in this the naval commander set up his headquarters, providing an additional signals link between the 9th Brigade and General Headquarters. After the capture of Sharm el Sheikh, he provided a shuttle service of seaborne supply with his landing craft between the troops there and the Port of Elath.

This concludes the story of the opening of the Gulf of Aqaba. There had been an alternative plan, if the opposition had been resolute at Dahab, to load an assault force into landing craft at Nuweiba and put them ashore at Dahab for a night attack. Unhappily for the Navy, but happily for everyone else, there was no need to put this plan into effect.

It was not until the end of November that my Piper Cub flew me to Sharm el Sheikh, low along the route taken by the 9th Brigade. We followed the track all the way, often with the mountains overtopping us on either side. It was almost impossible to believe that a brigade on wheels had gone that way three weeks earlier.

At Sharm el Sheikh the Army was busy fishing, with flippers on their feet and goggles over their eyes, for the marvelous shells that are to be found here and the lumps of coral. I was given a bed by the area commander in his room, which had formerly belonged to the Egyptian naval commander of the district.

It was the evening of the first day of Chanukah, the Jewish festival which lasts a week and which commemorates the military victories of Judas Maccabaeus. During the week a candlestick stands prominently in every house, not the seven-branched Menorah, the emblem of the state, but one with eight branches (a symbol of the miracle of eight days' oil in the Apocrypha)—one candle being lit each night until, at the end, all eight of them burn brightly—as a token and memorial of what can be done by warlike men in the cause of freedom with the help of God.

As we sat down to dinner in the area commander's mess and opened our tins of pressed beef and peas, the chief rabbi of the forces walked in with a miniature candlestick which he set on the table. We all covered our heads while we sang the Chanukah hymn:

> Rock of our strength, our redoubt,
> To whom praise for victory is due,
> Let us but rebuild the Temple
> And there make thank-offerings.

The chief rabbi of the forces seemed to be a relatively young man with a thick black beard and spectacles, behind which his eyes had a trace of fanatical glitter. He had a great sense of humor and, apart from his scholarly qualifications, was a trained paratrooper. For his first drop he composed a special prayer. Never before, he admitted, had he uttered a prayer with such fervor. For a short while I became his target. With tolerant ferocity he condemned, for its laxity, the London synagogue to which my family and I have belonged for the last four generations.

After dinner the night began to get cool. I put on a jersey and sat on the steps of the mess, looking across the gulf. Somebody gave me an English book which had been left behind by an Egyptian naval officer. It was a copy of Somerset Maugham's novel *Theatre*—not one of his best—which had been republished for international consumption under the title of *Woman of the World*. On the cover was a vivid picture of the woman of the world losing her virtue and most of her dress.

It was one of those strange evenings when, miles away from anywhere, all sorts of odd acquaintances come popping up from long-range memories, for a few words, greetings, questions-and-answers, then to vanish again into the darkness. A voice behind me asked, "How's Richmond Terrace these days?" Richmond Terrace was the site of Combined Operations Headquarters where I had served for a sizable part of our last war. A little later somebody sat down beside me and said, "I can't remember the name of the hotel where we met in Catania."

The next morning, as the first burning gash showed through the clouds over Saudi Arabia across the gulf, we took to the air again. After flying over Mount Sinai, we landed at an airstrip on the Gulf of Suez. While they were refueling our plane, an officer came up and said that he had something very interesting to show me. He hauled me into a truck which held several massive lumps of red sandstone from the Sinai Mountains, exquisitely carved with ancient Egyptian hieroglyphics, and another with the head of a woman, and another with "two trunkless legs," all in superb condition. The man said, "I'm sure I know your face." We found that we had served in the commandos together. We opened a tin of sardines to celebrate.

Then a Piper Cub took me back into the Sinai Mountains for a four-hour tour northward to look at the Monument and the Mitla Passes, and eastward along the way taken by the airborne brigade, but in reverse, and northward again to Kuseima, and back over the Israel frontier. It was very rough. I was nearly sick. It was very hot, and in a Piper Cub a tall man cannot divest himself of his flying jacket. I had cramp and a stomach ache. I was in Tel Aviv in time for lunch. The bar at the Dan Hotel was much the same as usual.

VII

The Battles of the Center

THERE are two sides to every battle. One side is laundered and starched by memories of courage and endurance, by *"de mortuis nihil nisi bonum,"* and by an understanding of the fog of war and of the human brain struggling to be decisive in the clutch of high explosives; by understanding and compassion we make that side of the battle look good and neat. The other side is the seamy side. I am looking mainly at the seamy side of the battles which took place in the central sector.

According to the plan, there were two main jobs to be done in the central sector by the Central Task Force (CTF). In Phase I it had to take Kuseima and be ready to send reinforcements to Mitla. Phase II was the pause of twenty-four hours. And in Phase III the CTF had to attack the southern apex of Egypt's defensive Triangle at the same time as the Northern Task Force was attacking the eastern apex. This was the plan. It was not followed very closely.

The CTF consisted of two infantry brigades—which I shall call, respectively, the northern infantry brigade and the southern infantry brigade—and an armored brigade. Of these forces, the southern infantry brigade was earmarked to take Kuseima in Phase I and to be ready to reinforce the Mitla operations; while the northern infantry brigade and the armored brigade were earmarked to take the very formidable defenses at Abu Aweigila in Phase III.

The operations of CTF started according to plan. The southern infantry brigade got to El Auja at two o'clock on the afternoon of D-Day. At this point it had to turn south along the track to Sabha, while the rest of CTF would, in due course, carry on westward along the main road to Abu Aweigila and ultimately to the canal at Ismailia.

As soon as the southern brigade turned southward, the civilian buses in which it was traveling ran into difficulties on account of the patches of soft sand along this indifferent route. At Sabha, which was unoccupied, the brigade had to take to its feet. This was at three o'clock in the afternoon, and Kuseima had to be taken before morning. Although it was only ten miles farther on, those miles consisted of very thick, deep sand which is some of the most tiring terrain imaginable for men on foot. And the men of the southern brigade—and of the northern brigade also—were mainly townsfolk, mobilized only three days previously, not particularly fit, by the standards of regular troops, and with an average age of over thirty. I am not sure how far these factors, topographical and human, had been appreciated in the CTF plan, according to which the southern infantry brigade should have been on its starting line, ready to attack Kuseima, by midnight.

The leading battalion of the southern infantry brigade took eleven hours to plod through the 10 miles of heavy sand between Sabha and Kuseima. By eleven o'clock on the night of D-Day it was clear to the CTF commander that the southern infantry brigade was going to be at least two hours late on its starting line. He began to get anxious. Kuseima was one of those places which, if it were not taken under cover of darkness, might put up a stubborn resistance by daylight. And the capture of Kuseima was of course an urgent essential. For this reason the CTF commander, ordered his armored brigade, which was back at El Auja, to put one armored combat team in "immediate readiness" to come to the Kuseima area.

This may seem a strange procedure. The Kuseima positions had been prepared on two small hills standing to the east of the road junction and were manned by only two infantry companies.

The Battles of the Center

The southern infantry brigade ought to have been able to take the positions without the help of armor. But this brigade was equipped with only two-wheel-drive civilian transport and had no means of getting to Kuseima except on foot.

At two o'clock in the morning—two hours late—the leading battalion attacked the Kuseima position. By four o'clock the first of the two hills had been captured, but the second was still holding out, and there was only another hour of darkness ahead. It was then that the CTF commander ordered the armored combat team, which had been put in readiness for this purpose, to come up. An hour after he had done so, the southern infantry brigade took the second hill; and when the Egyptians put in a counter-attack with a force of fighting jeeps, it was broken by the brigade reconnaissance company with its own fighting jeeps and half-tracks. The road junction at Kuseima was now in Israel's hands, which meant that the airborne brigade at Mitla could be reinforced from this direction and was safe against catastrophe. By now, however, the armored combat team had reached Kuseima, although it had not been used in the engagement.

The road junction at Kuseima is on flat ground behind its two protective hills. Here there was once a hamlet, and there are still a few houses, a cluster or two of palm trees, and a refreshing feeling of vegetation. Nobody has lived there for some years, except the two companies of Egyptian soldiers who were manning that military outpost.

From Kuseima the road runs northwestward through a fairly narrow pass which is very easily defensible and supposedly would be defended. On the other side of the pass there is open ground again, a flat plain. And the commander of CTF, when he reached Kuseima, was obviously bound to reconnoiter forward and discover whether or not the pass immediately in front of him was held, and, if so, in what sort of strength. It took him a very short time to learn that the Egyptian detachments were retreating very rapidly down the pass in front of the Israeli reconnaissance. The next step was obvious. The southern brigade, together with the armored combat team, was sent forward through the pass to the open plain beyond it.

On this open ground the road forked. One arm went due northward to Um Sheham (which was in fact the Abu Aweigila position) while the other arm led southwestward to Nakhl and Mitla. This second arm ran beneath a ridge of high, sometimes precipitous hills, broken by a pass called the Daika. If you followed the Nakhl road for about 10 miles, you would find the Daika on your right, leading northwestward; and if you followed the Daika, you would come out eventually on the main Ismailia road at the back of Abu Aweigila.

The point was, you would not expect to be able to follow the Daika Pass. It was real story-book stuff—about a hundred yards wide, and sometimes even less, with hills rising precipitously on each side. The track had been prepared for demolition in many places, and the walls of the pass had been prepared for defense. The pass at Daika was quite as formidable as the one at Mitla. Presumably it would be defended? But if by any chance it was *not* . . .

Standing at that road junction in mid-November, I tried to imagine the scene as it was at eleven o'clock on the morning of D plus 1, exactly a fortnight earlier. How would it have seemed? The campaign had just begun; we were well into enemy territory; the Egyptians had been running away in front of us; behind us was a whole infantry brigade and, what was more, an armored combat team, a third of an armored brigade. The armor ought not to have been there, but it was. The sight of it would have suggested to me all kinds of possibilities. The sight of armor excites me in the same way as a pack of foxhounds or a curling covey of partridges. If I had been the CTF commander at that moment . . .

It was at that moment that the CTF commander, standing at this road junction, was joined by Brigadier Simhoni. Simhoni was the commander of Southern Command, a very gallant and resourceful officer who has since been killed in an airplane accident.

The Battles of the Center

In the course of the conference that followed his arrival, it occurred to somebody that if the whole armored brigade could be got up the Daika that night it could attack Abu Aweigila in the rear, that is, from the west, while the northern infantry brigade was attacking from the east. By these means the position could be taken a day earlier than the plan provided.

In any event, it seemed that the armor would be better placed at this road junction, west of Kuseima, than back at El Auja. From here it would have a choice of several routes, either southwestward toward Nakhl and Mitla or northwestward to the central axis. There was everything to be gained and nothing to be lost by bringing it forward. Accordingly, the rest of the armored brigade was moved up from El Auja to the Kuseima area, and the leading armored combat team was told to send a reconnaissance unit into the Daika.

At four o'clock on that afternoon of D plus 1, news came back from the reconnaissance team in the Daika. Incredible as it seemed, the pass was being evacuated and the demolitions were being blown, about five hundred yards in front of the leading reconnaissance vehicles. In fact these demolitions were quite ineffective. They would not delay a military vehicle at all. But in the Egyptian mind, the mere fact of blowing a crater in the road was an assurance that the road was blocked. They had blown a bridge also. A blown bridge can give a lot of trouble when there is water underneath it, but none at all when the wadi that it crosses is dry and can be easily traversed. This was the case with the bridge at Daika.

On getting this news from Daika, the CTF commander issued new orders to his armored brigade. The brigade was to leave a battalion blocking the road—the right-hand fork—which led into the Abu Aweigila positions; it was to send one armored combat team to Bir Hasana, whence it could move swiftly either southwest to Mitla or north to the central axis. And the rest of the brigade was to go through the Daika by night and to attack the Abu Aweigila positions in the rear at daybreak.

Now none of this was very much according to the General Headquarters plan. It was all happening on D plus 1, which was Phase II, during which there was supposed to be the twenty-four-hour "pause." The plan seems to have been rather forgotten by somebody. Instead of a "pause" in which to test Egypt's reaction before deciding what next to do, here was Israeli armor taking advantage of what seemed to be a fleeting opportunity. Instead of taking the Abu Aweigila positions from the east with two brigades —the armored brigade and the northern infantry brigade—by dawn on D plus 3, CTF now proposed to take it a day earlier by simultaneous attacks in front and rear.

There seemed to be great advantages in this new plan. As soon as the armored brigade was through the Daika, it would have penetrated deep into the interior of the peninsula and would be astride the central axis to Ismailia. It might even get to that vital area around Bir Gifgafa—where the Germans had advised Nasser to site his main defenses—whence all the Egyptian forces in the peninsula could be virtually cut off. Yet, despite its brave prospects, the new plan had two dangers.

First, if the Abu Aweigila positions survived the simultaneous attacks in front and rear, there would be no chance of reverting to the original intention of launching a deliberate attack against those positions from the east. There was now nothing left to the east except the northern infantry brigade, which, with very little artillery, and without the support of armor, would have a hard job taking the position against anything like a resolute defense.

Second, although it would be a fine thing to get the armored brigade astride the central axis by way of the Daika, it might not be too easy to keep it supplied thereafter. Until Abu Aweigila was taken, and the main road opened from Israel's frontier, the armored brigade could be supplied only by the long and difficult route from El Auja to Sabha, to Kuseima, and thence northward through the Daika. Was it possible to keep the armor supplied along these tracks until such time as the Abu Aweigila positions had fallen?

The commanders conferring at Kuseima had come to the conclusion that it was.

In reaching this conclusion they were perhaps influenced by the lack of opposition that had so far been encountered and by the speed with which Kuseima, and the pass to the west of it, and the Daika itself, had been abandoned. What they did not know at that time—and indeed nobody knew till later—was that the Egyptians had two different words for expressing "defense." The first meant "to observe and to delay the enemy"; and the second meant defense in the British sense—"to hold to the last man and the last round." According to the Egyptian orders, everything to the south of the Abu Aweigila positions was to be defended only in the first sense, but the Abu Aweigila positions themselves were to be defended in the second.

While there was never much question of any Egyptian unit's defending anything in the second sense—"to the last man and the last round"—it was obvious that, if an Egyptian commander was told to defend something only in the first sense, it was a license to withdraw at the first signs of trouble. The fact that the Egyptians had done just this in the passes of Kuseima and Daika may have misled some of the Israeli commanders into thinking that the same thing might well happen at Abu Aweigila.

Abu Aweigila was once a village but, in recent times, had been turned into a military camp. A few kilometers southeast of the town there stands, now alone in the desert, a white and elegant villa beside a splendid dam, both of them the work of a great British administrator, Claude Scudamore Jarvis. Jarvis built his dam to bring prosperity to the district; and in this very pleasant villa he spent some years of his life. Nowadays the dam is unserviceable and the villa partly wrecked.

Abu Aweigila itself is indefensible, since it lies on perfectly flat ground and is commanded by higher ground to the east and the south. The defenses of the place were sited in depth, between three

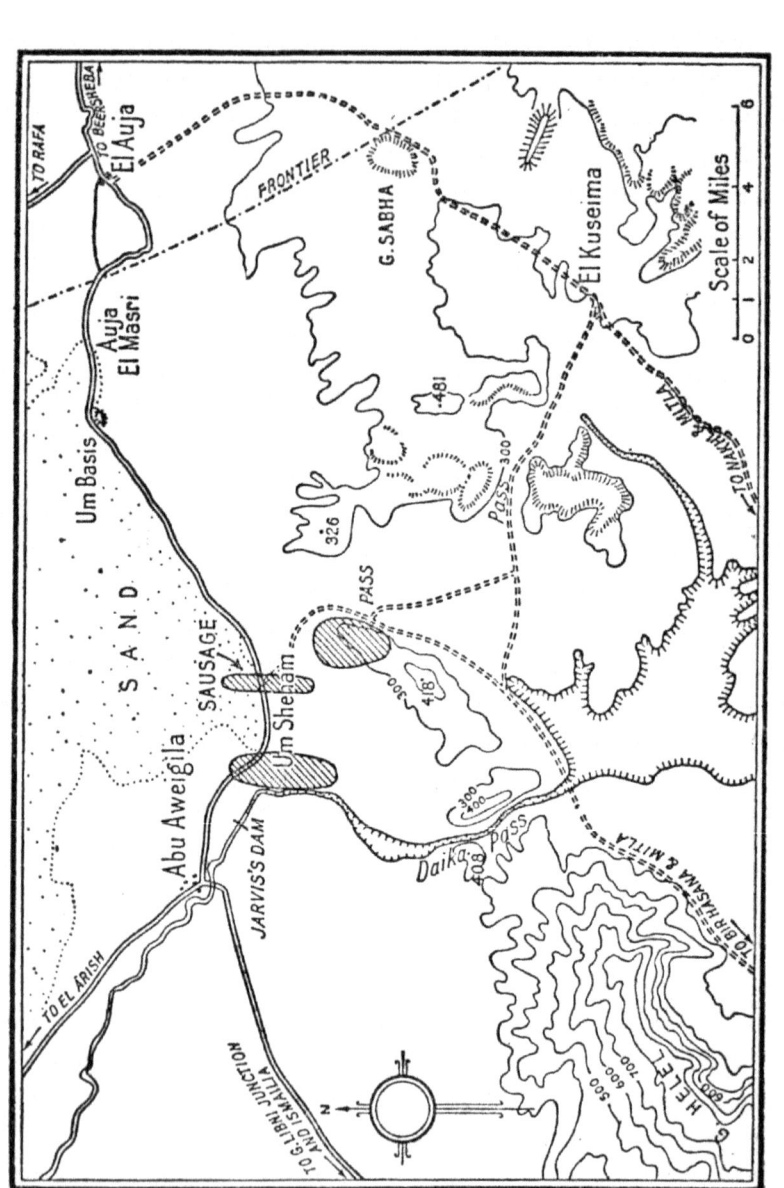

The Battle for Um Sheham in the Central Sector

and six miles to the east and southeast, in an area known as Um Sheham. Here there was an elaborate series of strong points, built on the higher ground and composed of mine fields, barbed wire, and emplacements for artillery, anti-tank guns, and machine guns. Their German designer concluded, with good reason, that these positions could scarcely be attacked from the north, where there is nothing but many miles of thick sand, impassable by either wheeled or tracked vehicles. To the south there is a chain of steep, rocky hills; and to the west, of course, lay Suez and Egypt. The greater part of these defenses were sited to shoot eastward, although there were also positions built on a narrow spur above Jarvis's villa and the dam, facing westward, and ready to engage any forces that might get to the rear of the main defenses.

In the midst of the Um Sheham positions there is a road junction, like a V, opening to the east. The upper arm of the V leads into Israel through hills at Um Basis and El Auja; and the southern arm of the V leads down to Kuseima. (This was the road that was now blocked by a detached battalion of the armored brigade.)

I have flown over and around Um Sheham and have walked through many of the defenses, looking at them from the point of view of both those who were to hold them and those who were to take them. They are formidable. The sand to the north is truly thick, very difficult for infantry and virtually impassable for wheels or even tracks. To the west the defenses rest upon that ridge, above Jarvis's villa, overlooking the valley that runs to Abu Aweigila itself. To the south they look down into the open plain and the positions where the battalion of the armored brigade was now entrenched. And to the east, where the main road entered from the Israel frontier, they completely commanded an open plain for a distance of about 3 miles, or 5000 yards, before running up to a ridge behind which the attacking force could get cover for the deployment of its infantry and for its artillery positions.

This distance is significant. Five thousand yards is the maximum range of the 120-mm. heavy mortar, which comprises a part of

Israel's artillery. On account of the range, the heavy mortars could not be used to support infantry attacking from the east.

The night of D plus 1 went according to the new plan. The northern brigade crossed the frontier so that the infantry could dig itself in on the ridge facing Um Sheham, with the artillery behind it. As for the armor, the combat team which had been sent to Bir Hasana got there without making contact with the enemy; and the remainder, less the battalion which was left blocking the southern entrance to Um Sheham, moved through the Daika Pass.

This armored brigade had a very remarkable commander. I am told by unbiased females of both British and American nationalities that there is no film star in Hollywood handsome enough to compare with him. I am no judge of such matters and can only say that from a military point of view he is an ideal type of armored commander. A quick, slim man, he speaks curtly, softly, sardonically. His sand goggles are on his forehead under his black beret, and he gets into his jeep, pulls down his goggles, and drives off across the desert in one smooth movement. He does so in a leisurely, almost languid way; but if you happen to be his passenger—as I was—you must leap for your seat like a startled rabbit, or the jeep will have gone without you. We will say that this officer's name was Benjamin. In Hebrew the J is pronounced like a Y and the last syllable is long and soft; so that the name sounds like Benyameen.

By dawn Benyameen's armor was through the Daika Pass and had reached Abu Aweigila, which was attacked instantly. It was taken with very little opposition. Benyameen would have immediately exploited this success with an attack on the rear of the Um Sheham positions, as planned, if he had not been told to wait until nine o'clock for an air attack on Um Sheham which had been ordered the previous night. In fact the air attack was never made; and when, after a few hours of waiting, Benyameen was told that it had been canceled, he redeployed his armor. One armored combat team was sent westward to Jebel Libni to block the road from Ismailia against reinforcements from Egypt; and a reconnaissance team was sent northward toward El Arish, with orders to keep off the road and to remain hidden. During the day it was able to report numerous attempts to reinforce Um Sheham from El Arish; these were engaged by Benyameen—who now had very little armor in hand—and turned back.

It seems almost certain, however, that Um Sheham had been reinforced already, notably by a number of anti-tank "Archers" which during the night had dug themselves into the ridge above Jarvis's dam. In addition, the Egyptian forces that had withdrawn without serious losses from Kuseima, and without fighting from the passes of Kuseima and of Daika, had all collected inside the Um Sheham perimeter.

If the original plan had been followed, the Egyptian command would still be wondering where the next Israeli attack was to be expected. But the various troop movements that had taken place the previous day—the day earmarked for the "pause"—and the considerable movement of Israeli armor, must have warned the Um Sheham garrison that it was soon to be assaulted. On this one occasion the Egyptian defenders were not taken by surprise, nor rushed off their feet, but were allowed time to prepare themselves mentally and physically for battle. And when the northern brigade put in a light attack with its reconnaissance company and an infantry company in half-tracks, at ten o'clock that morning, it met heavy artillery fire and was forced to withdraw.

It was now clear that a deliberate attack in strength would have to be launched against Um Sheham. It was decided to do so that night. This was the night of D plus 2—the time at which the attack should have been made, according to the original plan. CTF had got back to the original plan so far as timing was concerned; but instead of attacking with two brigades—one armored and one infantry—CTF had now only the northern brigade available. And of this brigade, one battalion had to be left entrenched

A fighting jeep in the brigade reconnaissance company

as a "firm base," covering the artillery positions behind it and the road to Israel. There were only two infantry battalions available for the attack.

But what about Benyameen's armor? It had been sent up the Daika in order to attack Um Sheham in the rear while the northern brigade was making a frontal assault. But the chance had now been missed. Benyameen's attention had been diverted elsewhere. During the morning of D plus 2 the 1st Egyptian Armored Brigade had come across the canal and was advancing down the central axis. The reports said that its leading elements were already at Bir Hama, scarcely 30 miles from Abu Aweigila. If Benyameen's armor had still been on the eastern side of Abu Aweigila, this would have been good news. The greater the Egyptian forces that could be drawn into the battle, the greater would be the defeat of the Egyptian Army—always providing the battle was won. And the winning of the battle at Um Sheham might depend on Benyameen's armor's supporting the northern brigade's attack.

But Benyameen was not in a position to support the northern brigade; nor was he safely to the east of Abu Aweigila; he was out on a limb west of Abu Aweigila, where his only supply line was long, circuitous, and fragile; and the Egyptian armor was, according to the reports, not 30 miles off. Benyameen had to act quickly. To meet the Egyptian armor he prepared a trap for it on the hammer-and-anvil principle. The anvil was to be the armored combat team which was already at Jebel Libni; the hammer was to be the other armored combat team, which was at Bir Hasana, some fifteen miles to the south of the main road, and which was now ordered to move northward.

The trap was laid, but it remained unsprung for the rest of the day, because the report about the Egyptian armor was inaccurate; the armor was not at Bir Hama, at all, but 20 miles farther to the west at Bir Gifgafa, where it was attacked and severely punished by the Israel Air Force. By air action alone it was temporarily disabled for the rest of that day. But Benyameen was not aware of this at the time. And even if he had suspected it, he could not have ignored the presence of the Egyptian armor; he could not have turned his back on it, in order to attack Um Sheham in the rear.

Nevertheless Benyameen did what he could. By late afternoon he had very little of his force in hand, but he decided to attack Jarvis's dam at sunset with everything that he could scrape up. This consisted of a single company of Sherman tanks (in all armies a company or squadron consists of 15 tanks, or something less) and an infantry company in half-tracks. These would have to advance across 2 miles of flat ground which was completely commanded by the ridge above the dam. Dug into this ridge there were now some 12 "Archers" and 13 57-mm. anti-tank guns. Properly manned, they should have held up an armored division.

Benyameen launched his modest attack with the sun behind him at the moment of sunset. He finished it in darkness with the searchlights of some of his tanks blazing. The half-tracks carrying his infantry got left behind, and only his company of Shermans moved against those 25 anti-tank guns. He took the position with the temporary loss of half his tanks, all but two of which were

A Sherman tank

repaired and operational again by the next morning. But the infantry who were following took heavy punishment, losing 6 of their half-tracks and having 75 casualties, of whom 7 were dead.

The fringe of the Um Sheham positions had now been breached from the rear, although Benyameen had nothing left with which to exploit his success. A little later he scraped up a few more tanks and deployed them in hull-down positions on the eastern side of the ridge above the dam, where they could command the main road running through the enemy's defenses. Here they remained until the end of the battle and did much damage.

While Benyameen was attacking from the west, the northern infantry brigade was to have attacked from the east with its two infantry battalions supported by one artillery battalion of twenty-

The Battles of the Center

five-pounders and a medium battery. Against any reasonable defense this force would be inadequate. By British or American standards, an attack from this direction upon these positions would not have been attempted without the support of at least a divisional artillery amounting to perhaps six times the fire-power that CTF had available. Acording to the original plan, the fire-power to support this attack should have been provided by Benyameen's tanks.

The situation was now tricky. Fuel and ammunition could be got to Benyameen only by the circuitous and difficult route through Sabha, Kuseima, and Daika. These tracks were getting worse and worse and, from the point of view of supplies carried in civilian lorries, might shortly collapse. To relieve this problem, it was now urgent to take Um Sheham and to open the direct road from El Auja to Benyameen's armor.

The two battalions of the northern infantry brigade which had to take Um Sheham that night were to attack alongside each other, on the southern side of the road, with 2nd Battalion on the right and 1st Battalion on the left. (These are pseudonyms.) They were to take the sausage-shaped position—known as "Sausage"—which lay astride the main road with its left or northern flank resting on the thick, soft sand which was impassable to wheels or tracks.

From the start, everything went wrong with this brigade attack. 1st Battalion, which had moved to its starting line the previous night and had rested during the day, was in good shape. But 2nd Battalion, which was not moved until late that afternoon, never succeeded in getting to its starting line at all. Some miles short of it, its civilian buses got stuck in soft sand and could go no farther. And the time was now too late for the battalion to dismount and proceed on foot. It was therefore ordered to return to the main road, to de-bus there, and to make a wide circuit under cover of darkness, so that it could attack Sausage from the north.

Since this area was impassable to vehicles, 2nd Battalion had to leave its support company behind it. Moreover, by one of those freaks of ordnance which occur even in the best-regulated armies, the "carriers," by which an infantryman can hump his heavy weapons on his back, had been withdrawn for modification some weeks previous and had not been returned on mobilization. The battalion, therefore, had to make this attack without either mortars or medium machine guns—a deficiency which was of little account that night, but was sorely felt the next morning.

Meanwhile, 1st Battalion was held up on the left. It had no sooner started out than it became heavily engaged by an unknown and unexpected enemy position which had been missed by the Israel intelligence. This position kept the battalion from advancing farther until eleven o'clock the next morning, when it was finally taken. It was then found to have been held by one infantry company.

At midnight, then, while 1st Battalion was thus engaged, 2nd Battalion was still struggling through the thick sand dunes on its northern route toward Sausage. It was being supported by fire from all the artillery that the force possessed. Its leading elements, including the battalion commander and his artillery officer, had reached the edge of the Sausage perimeter, and the rest were somewhere behind them in the darkness. On the supposition that the attack would shortly be ready to go in, the artillery were ordered to stop firing on the immediate objective. In fact it was not until four hours later, an hour before dawn, that the attack could finally be launched.

By then, it had been decided to help 2nd Battalion by mounting a new attack from the east with two companies in half-tracks that had been sent up from reserve. They formed up and charged straight across the open ground, with headlights blazing, at the most heavily defended face of the Sausage position.

This was a technique that had been successfully employed in reprisal raids such as those at Husan and Kalkilyah. The trick had also worked with the airborne brigade against Thamed, which had been held by two detached infantry companies. But Um Sheham was another matter. Here there was a whole infantry brigade en-

The Battles of the Center

trenched with very large numbers of anti-tank guns covering barbed wire and mine fields, and there was no element of surprise. There was not even a sunrise or a sunset behind the charge to dazzle the defenders. There were only the headlights presenting an unmistakable target: a long line of half-tracks advancing across three miles of open plain. Most of the half-tracks were destroyed instantly; there were 90 casualties; the commander was killed, and his second-in-command was wounded.

Meanwhile 2nd Battalion in the north had pushed home its attack and, with great resolution, had got inside the perimeter. Once there, however, it was subjected to very heavy fire from artillery and mortars which, according to the German doctrine and timing, were ranged and ready to fire on any part of their own defenses that might be captured. After suffering more than 50 casualties, 2nd Battalion was forced back into the sand dunes.

It was now daylight, and the battalion continued to receive heavy punishment from artillery and mortars. Lacking its support company, it had nothing with which to reply. It was therefore ordered to withdraw, back through 3 miles of thick sand-dunes, until it reached the cover of the ridge. That night's fighting had been costly, and by noon the following day nothing had been gained but the capture of the one isolated position that had been held by one Egyptian company. And the central axis, the main road to Ismailia, was not yet open.

By that time—noon on D plus 3—the general situation had changed radically. Rafa had been captured that morning, and an armored brigade was already exploiting westward toward El Arish. Benyameen, with his armor, was coping most satisfactorily with the Egyptian armor along the road to Ismailia, and the latter was being subjected to continuous air attacks. And Benyameen was in control of those vital uplands around Bir Gifgafa, from which area it would very shortly be possible to cut off the escape of all the Egyptian forces in the Sinai Peninsula.

These forces now comprised a very large proportion of the whole Egyptian Army. In addition to the troops which were stationed in Sinai before the operations began, Egypt had sent as reinforcements the 1st Armored Brigade, the 1st Mobile Infantry Brigade (known as the "German Brigade" on account of its German instructors), and the 3rd Infantry Brigade. To the west of the canal there remained only two infantry brigades (the 7th and 8th), and two armored brigades, of which one was still in process of formation. One day more of the campaign—perhaps only a dozen hours—and there would be very little left of the Egyptian Army.

But the Anglo-French bombing had just started. General Headquarters in Cairo recalled all Egyptian formations and units which were not yet irrevocably committed, and the 1st Mobile Infantry Brigade and 3rd Infantry Brigade were extricated safely. It was a great pity. They were arriving on the scene just after the decisive battle at Rafa had been won; they would have been just in time to be neatly routed.

I have let myself run a little ahead of the narrative of the Central Task Force. During the afternoon of D plus 3, while Um Sheham was sealed, it was subjected to air attack. Until nightfall four Mustangs were kept in the air continuously over the positions, subjecting them to bombs, rockets, and strafing. After dark, and throughout the night, all units of the CTF reported organized attempts by the enemy to break out of Um Sheham in all directions. When morning came, there seemed to be a strange calm over the whole area. At nine o'clock that morning, the CTF Commander ordered a battalion and a company of tanks, with artillery and air support, to advance toward the position. No shot was fired at it. It entered the Um Sheham fortifications and met no resistance. All the enemy weapons and artillery were in position and intact—but there was not a soul about.

The tank commander then met an Egyptian jeep which was flying a white flag and was driven by an Egyptian soldier bringing a message. The message was written in English, the language common to both Egyptian and Israeli troops, and had been sent by Benyameen to the Egyptian commander of Um Sheham, advising him to surrender instantly or be annihilated. This message never reached the Egyptian commander. The Egyptian prisoner who was bearing it had driven right through the Um Sheham positions from Abu Aweigila and had come out the other side! It was learned later that at dusk the previous night the Egyptian officers had assembled all their men and had given them orders amounting to *"sauve qui peut,"* every man for himself. The whole force was to abandon its weapons, to disperse, and to make its way home in individual groups as best it could. This was the meaning of the repeated attempts to break out during the previous night.

The fate of the Um Sheham garrison during its flight through the desert was terrible. The terrain which it had to cross is of thick, undulating sand on which even walking was a dreadful endurance. It is of course completely waterless; and for mile after mile there is no scrub, not even a thorn bush, nor any scrap of vegetation.

Israel's air reconnaissance saw the terrible spectacle of these men, crazy with thirst and falling from exhaustion, dying in the desert—with the Bedouin falling upon them and cutting their throats for the sake of their clothing. There was nothing that Israel could do to save them. No vehicle could be sent to their assistance, because none could get through those sand dunes. Out of the 3000 men who had been manning the Um Sheham defenses, some 700 were taken prisoner by Israel. It is doubtful if a single one of the remainder got back to Egypt or escaped death in the desert from either thirst or the Bedouin.

This was the end of the Üm Sheham battle. Since it was the only engagement in the whole campaign in which Israel failed to achieve a spectacular victory, it was probably the most useful in terms of military teaching.

During the Um Sheham battle, Benyameen was hunting his main quarry, which was the Egyptian armor. The hammer-and-anvil trap at Jebel Libni had been in vain, because 1st Egyptian Armored Brigade halted its advance eastward and turned south from Bir Gifgafa toward the Monument, thus threatening the airborne brigade in the south. To meet this threat, Benyameen ordered the combat team which had advanced northward from Bir Hasana to retrace its steps and meet the Egyptian armor in the area of the Monument, where the terrain was ideal for armored warfare. Again this combat team was to be the hammer, but this time the airborne forces in their entrenched positions were to be the anvil. It will be remembered, from Chapter V, the desperate efforts that had been made by the airborne brigade to prepare for this contingency during the previous night.

The armored battle at the Monument never took place, because the 1st Egyptian Armored Brigade turned back once more to the main Ismailia road which was to be its graveyard. Benyameen met it during the early afternoon of D plus 3. It was his encounter with the Russian T.34s, and he promptly destroyed 8 of them without any losses to himself. Although the Russian tanks had the better armament—and indeed were better in almost every respect than Israel's Shermans—their Egyptian crews never succeeded in getting in the first shot. In tank warfare it is the first shot that counts—provided it is accurate.

Subjected to constant air attack, and harassed by Benyameen, these Egyptian tanks had a hard time of it. Dressed in a pink coat and a hunting cap, Benyameen would make a typical master and amateur huntsman of a fashionable pack of foxhounds somewhere in the English Midlands. He hunted down those tanks till none were left. On one occasion, when his own vehicle was temporarily out of action, he got into an Egyptian tank and used it instead. Quite often the Egyptians quitted their tanks intact and left them with the engines running.

On the night of D plus 3, Benyameen got a message that some scores of enemy tanks were dug in near Bir Gifgafa. He planned a coordinated attack against them to be launched at dawn from both the east and south. To carry it out, the combat team that had moved toward the Monument came up through the "impassable sand" which had been the Egyptian excuse for withdrawal. But at dawn on the morning of D plus 4, when the attack had been launched, nothing remained of these scores of tanks but a rear guard of four T.34s and four SU 100s. They were all captured or destroyed. The SU 100s—the latest thing in tank destroyers, straight from the Iron Curtain—surrendered themselves intact.

By now, most of Benyameen's tanks were temporarily out of action, in need of repair and maintenance. He gave orders that any of his armored vehicles that could still move were to carry on the pursuit with the utmost speed. Finally, during the morning of D plus 4, he himself reached the canal, opposite Ismailia, with a force of four of his own Shermans and four captured T.34s—which brought to a close and a conclusion the operations in the central sector.

VIII

Victory in the North

THE most impressive of Israel's victories in the whole campaign, and the most important, was won at Rafa by the Northern Task Force (NTF). I have left the operations of NTF until the last, not on chronological account—they were concluded before those of the 9th Brigade against Sharm el Sheikh had even started —but because they were decisive. Once Rafa had been taken, the defensive Triangle had been cracked at its northeastern apex, the Gaza Strip had been sealed and cut off from Egypt, and the way was open to El Arish and Qantara.

According to the original plan, Rafa and Um Sheham were to be attacked simultaneously in Phase III during the night of D plus 2. The attacks would therefore have reinforced each other. If either was held up, it could be helped by the success of the other: Um Sheham could be taken in the rear by way of Rafa and El Arish; or Rafa could be taken in the rear by way of Um Sheham and El Arish. It was a good, sound plan on orthodox principles.

This plan had been jeopardized when Benyameen's armor was sent through the Daika Pass and, in consequence, the Central Task Force was left with insufficient forces to be sure of taking Um Sheham by assault. This made it all the more imperative that the operations of NTF should be successful. If the attack on Rafa—which was just as tough a proposition as Um Sheham—had fared no better than the attack on Um Sheham, the situation of Israel on the morning of D plus 3 would not have been very good.

There was of course never the least possibility of her "losing the war," or anything of that sort; but the Sinai Campaign might have taken a week or more instead of a hundred hours, and would have been more costly. In that case, the Anglo-French intervention might have been to Israel's advantage, instead of the reverse.

According to the original plan, Rafa was to be taken by forces exactly similar to those allotted for the capture of Um Sheham—an armored brigade and an infantry brigade. But whereas CTF had an additional infantry brigade to use in Phase I for the reinforcement, if necessary, of the airborne brigade at Mitla, NTF had an additional infantry brigade to use in Phase IV for the final capture or occupation of Gaza. From this additional brigade, NTF had to detach one battalion for internal security duties against the fedayeen from Gaza, who, in the event of war, had orders to switch their attacks from civilian to military targets. And authority was also given for a second battalion from this brigade to be used in the attack on Rafa. For this purpose it was attached to the other infantry brigade.

Hence, the forces available to the NTF commander for the attack on Rafa consisted of one infantry brigade of four battalions and one armored brigade.

The commander of NTF had, on first encounter, a deceptive presence. He seemed to be a small man, with a cynical, almost scholarly expression. His temperament was taut, as if he were living on nervous energy and driving himself at high pressure. When he first came into the room (it was a social occasion) you felt the electrical waves of his unrest; but after a while in his company, you could feel with equal impact his sudden relaxation. Sometimes it seemed that he was trying to remain withdrawn, taking no part in the conversation, diverting his thoughts elsewhere. But his presence could not be ignored, and you found yourself launching your remarks in his direction. He is amongst the most brilliant of Israel's commanders, and—although he might deny, but not resent, the allegation—he is an Anglophile with a warm, humorous if cynical, affection for British ways, and especially for the British Army, with which he served during World War II. We will give him the name of David, which is pronounced in Hebrew with the "a" short, and the last syllable long and sweet—like "Doveed" or "Duveed." I should perhaps add that my impressions of Doveed were false in many respects. I have since been told that he is in fact a large man—larger than myself—and a very cool customer.

Doveed's plan was orthodox. The Rafa positions would be attacked from the east and would be pierced in their center by all his four infantry battalions advancing on parallel axes under cover of darkness. Shortly before dawn, his armored brigade was to advance on the right of the infantry, take the positions on its immediate front, and then swing left-handed ahead of the infantry brigade, or through its leading elements, and get on to the main coastal road to El Arish. It was then to move along this road as fast as it could.

Doveed realized that his principal difficulty would be the initial penetration of the positions by the infantry. Not only were the positions extremely strong, but they completely commanded the ground across which the infantry would have to advance for a distance which varied between 5 miles on the right of the infantry sector and 10 miles on the extreme left. The positions were too strong to be taken during daylight by the forces at his disposal. A daylight attack would need ten times the artillery he had got; and the obvious way of getting into the Rafa positions was by a night attack. Night attacks were of course a specialty of the Israeli Army.

A night attack on the extreme left of the infantry sector presented a particular problem. The distance of open ground which the infantry would have to cross was too great for them to leave their starting lines after dark, to advance on foot to the enemy wire, to penetrate the wire, to clear a lane through the mine fields, and to take their objectives before daylight. The obvious recourse would be to send the infantry forward during the previous night and to let them lie up during the following day in concealed posi-

A typical Egyptian machine-gun post

tions. But there were no concealed positions to be found in this area. There was no scrap of concealment, nor scarcely a fold in the ground, where the infantry could lie covered from fire, or even from observation, by daylight. Therefore Doveed had to send them into battle on wheels.

His plan, therefore, was that the two left-hand battalions, which had the greatest distance to go, should be transported as far as possible, at least to the edge of the enemy mine fields, by half-tracks and led by tanks; but that the two right-hand battalions, which had only about 5 miles of open ground to cover, should advance on foot. Furthermore, an attempt would be made by sappers to clear a lane through the mine fields the previous night. This preliminary operation had to be done in such a way that the enemy would not realize or discover it—or, if they did, would not interpret it correctly and realize precisely what was afoot. These mine fields, through which the infantry had to pass, were of course very fully covered by enemy cross-fire from several different positions.

The Egyptians and their German advisers had fully appreciated the double significance of Rafa as an apex of the defensive Triangle and also as the point at which the Gaza Strip could be sealed from Egypt. El Arish, which had been built up by the British, dur-

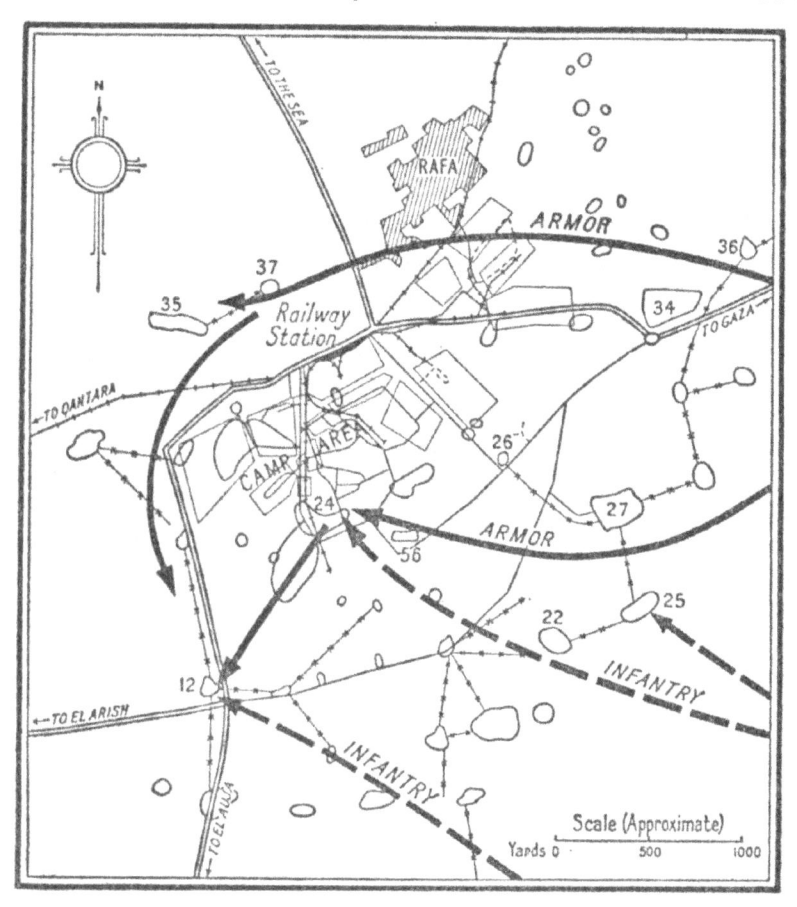

The Decisive Battle for Rafa

ing two world wars, into an Aldershot of the Middle East—as had Rafa also—was now an immense military base with workshops, ordnance depots, gasoline stores, and supplies deposited in huge quantities in preparation for the forthcoming campaign by Egypt against Israel. And Rafa, on which the defense of El Arish depended, had been strongly fortified and comprised a large number of mutually supporting positions, with emplacements and some concrete, each surrounded by several barbed-wire fences enclosing mine fields. They were manned by the 5th Egyptian Brigade, consisting of four battalions, with much additional artillery and many anti-tank guns.

Normally defended, these positions could not have been captured by a force less than three times, if not five times, the size of the force defending them. Yet the forces which Israel allotted for the capture of Rafa had a numerical superiority of less than two to one over the defenders; they had a smaller number of field guns, and only one battalion of medium artillery consisting of 8 155-mm. guns.

There were two factors which helped the NTF in this tough proposition. Since the operations were not to start until Wednesday night (the end of D plus 2), it had time to concentrate then without undue haste. It is true that part of this precious time had already been stolen by General Headquarters, since an advantage of staggering the start of operations was that mobilization could be staggered also, and hence the congestion on the roads and the strain on other Q facilities could be reduced. This was the first advantageous factor. The second was Udah.

Udah was the commander of the infantry brigade which was to attack on the left. He is a remarkable character. Again, my female advisers tell me that he is outstandingly handsome, or at least attractive. He is certainly very big, well proportioned, and almost ostentatiously tough. Women get the impression of ruthlessness, which, apparently, is an irresistible quality. His complexion is fair but of course weathered, and he is another of the blue-eyed Sabras, born in Israel of what is elsewhere called "humble parentage." At an early age he was earning money by carrying round the milk. His moods—at least in my company—alternated between almost savage impetuosity at high pressure and complete relaxation.

In the past he has held military appointments which are of supreme importance to any army and has done so with a very high measure of perception and shrewdness seasoned, they say, with a touch of Oriental cunning. During the day that I spent with him traveling amongst his troops through the very large area of which he was, by then, the military commander, I was left in no doubt that his men held him in the deepest devotion. Personally, if I were still a soldier, I should ask nothing more than to be one of his subordinates.

Udah's great achievement was not only to inspire the troops under his command with great resolution, but also to contrive somehow to keep tight control of what might have been a very difficult battle. Moreover he was able to keep a very intimate liaison with the commander of the armored brigade on his right—another splendid character who will appear a little later—and the very close cooperation of these two brigades was one of the outstanding features of the whole campaign.

On the night preceding the attack—that is to say, the night of D plus 1—Udah's sappers went forward, as planned, to open a way through the mine fields on the extreme left of his sector. It was an exceptionally dark night by Middle Eastern standards and Udah was not at all sure that they had succeeded. His doubts were reinforced by the sight, during the following day, of a number of Arabs moving through that same mine field. The distance was too great for their actions to be accurately observed; but it seemed possible not only that the mines were being replaced, but that the work of Udah's sappers had been detected and perhaps correctly interpreted.

There was nothing that Udah could do about it. At nightfall his infantry started to advance. The two battalions on the left were carried in half-tracks and led by tanks. At once the enemy artillery opened up, but the edge of the mine fields was reached with few casualties. It was then that the trouble started. Almost immediately the convoy ran into mines and came under very heavy fire from artillery, anti-tank guns, and machine guns. A half-track and a command car blew up, blocking the lane through the mine fields. The infantry dismounted and started to advance on foot, taking heavy casualties.

Meanwhile, the tanks and half-tracks, seeking a new lane through the mine fields, turned right. They made some progress in the dark night—it was again very dark—until the leading half-track blew up. Just when the whole convoy seemed to have been cut off in the mine field, the driver of a half-track was wounded and lost control of his vehicle, which careered away into the darkness until, at the farther edge of the mine field, it finally struck a mine. Although the driver was killed, the officer in charge was only wounded and was able to order the remainder of the convoy to follow his tracks and drive past him.

Once out of the mine field, the tanks and the half-tracks continued to move westward until, by good luck, they made contact once more with their own infantry. With the benefit of tank support and the use of their half-tracks, the infantry were able to secure all their objectives with little further opposition. These objectives consisted of a series of enemy positions extending back to the edge of Rafa itself. The last position that had to be taken, by the extreme left-hand battalion, enclosed an important road junction on the main coastal road from Gaza to El Arish. The capture of this position (marked number 12 on the map) was an essential preliminary to the advance of the armored brigade the next morning. The road passed through the middle of the perimeter, which consisted of several double-apron fences enclosing mine fields.

The battalion which took this position did so at daybreak by simultaneous attacks from the northeast and southeast. It was met by very heavy fire, and the northeasterly attack was stopped. It was then that the position was penetrated from the southwest by half-tracks, and instantly the whole defense collapsed. The road to El Arish was open, and the Egyptians took it. A few hours later it was carrying the leading elements of the armored brigade of NTF on their way to El Arish.

Meanwhile, the two right-hand battalions of Udah's brigade were having a tough time of it. They had less distance to go than the left-hand battalions—they had five miles of open ground to cover before they got to the enemy wire—but it had to be done on foot. For the last mile or more they were subjected to very heavy fire from artillery, mortars, and machine guns. When they came up against the enemy wire and mine fields this fire was maintained and increased at close range. What little support the artillery was able to give could not be very effective, because the enemy emplacements were dug deeply into the hillocks and heavily sandbagged. By first light, not one of these positions had been taken and, since the attackers now presented visible targets to an enemy at almost point-blank range, the situation began to look critical. Udah says he was worried—and it takes a good deal to worry Udah. He asked for help from the armored brigade on his right and he got it instantly.

One company commander who conducted me around the position he had taken explained to me how he did it: "Here we tried to get through the wire, but the Bangalore torpedo didn't go off and we were being shot at by that machine gun." (The range was under 100 yards.) "We were lucky to get a direct hit on it with a mortar, but then we were also being shot at by another machine gun from that other position on the right." (These two positions, on separate hills, were mutually supporting.) "Anyway, we couldn't get through the wire here and we were losing a lot of men, so we got round to the back of the position and found the way into it used by the Egyptians."

There were no less than five separate wire fences to be traversed from this direction, and the passage through them was in an irregular zig-zag, presenting a maze which I myself, on a peaceful morning, found difficult to navigate. The company commander continued: "After a bit, we got stuck on the wire; so some of our fellows lay across it while the others climbed over their backs. We had to stop our artillery from shooting because they were hitting us." (No wonder! The remnants of the company were in the rear of the enemy position in the direct line of artillery fire, and not more than 100 yards beyond it.) "So we got over the wire and took the position. Then we saw our armor spread out all over the country and coming up to help us. It was a wonderful sight."

It may have been noticed that I have been unable to describe these operations with the same degree of detail as those of other units in other sectors. In the first place, I had influenza at the time of this particular visit, and a temperature. In the second place, Udah was carting me across country at a pace which made it scarcely possible to take notes. His driver was put at the back of the jeep alongside the radio operators; he took the wheel himself; and I was sitting beside him in the seat he normally occupied, close by the automatic weapon which is mounted on these vehicles for anti-aircraft defense.

Udah, at the wheel, drove with one foot hard on the floor—the foot which was operating the accelerator pedal—and one hand almost permanently on the horn. The rest of our escort of jeeps followed as best it could. When we hit the road or traveled along it, everyone else sensibly made for the ditch. Udah was the military commander of this district.

On one occasion a conscientious military policeman signaled us to halt. Udah obeyed. As I hit the windshield the MP saluted smartly and said, "Shalom, Aluf Mishne." (An aluf mishne is a full colonel, which is the rank held by brigade commanders in Israel's Army.)

Udah replied, "Shalom." This is the traditional expression for salutation, welcome, and farewell; it means "peace," which I found reassuring, since the atmosphere was electrical and anything but peaceful. I could understand from his gestures that the MP was explaining to Udah the rules of the road—which were blatantly irrelevant. When he had finished, Udah let in the clutch, and I tumbled into the lap of the radio operator on the back seat.

We were through the sound barrier by the time we reached the outskirts of El Arish, and I was lucky to be still aboard when he turned suddenly left (the jeep has, of course, a left-hand drive) —at the entrance of Udah's headquarters. Here there was a sentry manning a chain across the drive. Our horn was sounding continuously; a truck ahead of us shot out of the way, and the sentry jumped clear. From forty miles an hour we dead-halted in the space reserved for the military commander's use. Like gunmen on a smash-and-grab affair, we dashed into his office. Then we sat down in comfortable chairs and chattered about nothing for twenty minutes.

It was, I think, contemporary art that we were discussing—Udah is an amateur painter, whose work has great charm and delicacy—when suddenly we did a "scramble" (a word which I use in a fighter airfield's technical sense) and found ourselves re-embarked, this time in Udah's own staff car of civilian pattern, and heading for the Suez Canal, which was scarcely 120 miles to the westward. After a mile, however, we suddenly swung right up a drive and stopped abruptly at an extraordinary white house which had a very narrow frontage but was several stories high.

Here we were greeted with huge delight in Arabic. The crowd which surrounded us were Arab residents of El Arish, and one of them was an excellent cook. He got his instructions, over Udah's shoulder, while we were led at frantic speed to the roof, there to repose ourselves for ten minutes, admiring the view, which was extensive and enchanting.

We finished our cigarettes, stumbled downstairs again, and found ourselves seated in the dining room. The meal which had been ordered only ten minutes previously consisted of five courses and was completed in the space of twenty minutes. The drill of the Arab squad seemed practiced and precise. Each course was on the table by the time we were halfway through its predecessor. It was the best meal that I have had in Israel, and I would have willingly spent an evening over it. But there was no time to waste.

Coffee had scarcely been put before us when we dashed back to the car which, by now, was being hosed down, scrubbed with soap, and polished by a posse of Arabs. Udah drove the car out of their clutches, shouting a word of praise as he went. One of the Arabs managed to get a final flick of his rag at our stern as we vanished back toward headquarters. Once more in Udah's office, we settled down to an hour of pleasant conversation while a very pretty girl in uniform fed us on glasses of tea and Egyptian biscuits.

Needless to say, Udah's infantry brigade secured all its objectives during the first few hours of daylight. Meanwhile, the armored brigade had entered the battle on his right.

This brigade was commanded by, shall we say, Isaac, which in Hebrew is pronounced so that it sounds like "Izzhak." Another of these blue-eyed Sabras, he seems almost permanently asleep. He has a soft and drowsy voice. On the rare occasions when he opens his eyes it is with a look of extraordinary penetration, as if he had discovered some horrible secret inside you which was very funny. Without the help of any of his features he seems to laugh. His ears stick out. He is of medium height, light, quick on his feet but leisurely in his movements.

As long as he possibly could, Izzhak avoided meeting me; and it was not until the end of my three weeks' research that I pinned him down at last. Danny assured me that there was nothing personal about his elusiveness, and certainly that he had nothing against the British—for whom he had acquired a considerable affection while attending the Senior Officers' School at Devizes— but only that he found it boring to narrate his armored adventures.

When at last I got to him, his boredom was very well disguised beneath a most hospitable welcome; there were glasses of tea and a cream cake which, as I bit it, exploded all over his maps and my notebook. He seemed to have all the time in the world to tell me the story of his brigade and he kept a considerate eye on my moving pencil.

Izzhak's armored brigade was divided, for tactical purposes, into three combat teams: CT(A), CT(B), and CT(C). The first two combat teams—CT(A) and CT(B)—were each composed of one tank squadron of Shermans and one infantry company in half-tracks. The third combat team—CT(C)—consisted of a squadron of AMXs, which is an excellent light-tank or tank destroyer, and an infantry company in half-tracks. In addition to these three combat teams, Izzhak had also a lorried infantry unit.

Operations started at two-thirty on the morning of D plus 3, Thursday, with an air bombardment which was to have lasted for thirty-five minutes. The aircraft experienced great difficulty in finding their target, and the bombardment took twice as long as had been expected, and was not effective.

From nightfall the armored brigade had been subjected to fire from enemy artillery, to which the Israel artillery was unable to respond since it had been ordered to keep silent until two o'clock in the morning, so that some element of surprise should remain and its battery positions should not be discovered. During those hours of silence its counter-battery units successfully located every single one of the enemy artillery positions, all of which, from two o'clock onward, were attacked by gunfire and temporarily silenced.

Forty minutes before first light—that is, at about four o'clock in the morning—the lorried infantry unit disembarked from its vehicles and advanced toward its objectives. Its task was to take positions 34 and 36, at the same time as Udah's infantry on the left were taking positions 24 and 25. The lorried infantry were no sooner afoot than they came under very heavy mortar fire, from which they lost 11 men killed and many wounded, and were unable to advance any farther. During the last few minutes of darkness, Izzhak sent CT(A) to their assistance.

The advance of CT(A) was the sight which had so stirred the infantry company commander when he was describing to me how he had taken position 25. CT(A), accompanied by Izzhak's second-in-command, passed through the lorried infantry unit and took positions 34 and 36. But it had been an expensive engagement, and the considerable casualties that it suffered included the infantry commander killed and Izzhak's second-in-command wounded. They had made the common mistake of traveling in the same vehicle, which was hit by a 57-mm. shell from a Russian anti-tank gun.

It was a fairly critical time all along the Rafa front. This was the moment when the infantry was held up, and Udah was asking the armor for help. In particular, position 27 had to be taken immediately. Izzhak ordered CT(B) forward. It advanced and made contact with the infantry, and between them they took position 27 in a few minutes. With the infantry riding on the tanks, they broke clean through all the positions in that vicinity and reached a junction of road and track that was still some distance from the main coastal road which had to be reached. Here the infantry were left to mop up and consolidate, and CT(B) stopped for refueling. By now a number of tanks and half-tracks had been lost by CT(A) and CT(B), half of them on mines, and the remainder from antitank fire, two being hit by bazookas. Accordingly Izzhak brought his light tanks of CT(C) up the road from reserve.

For a layman like myself in matters of armored warfare, it is not easy to appreciate the limitations which are imposed on tanks by the need to refuel and replenish their ammunition. Although a tank has a wide range in terms of miles, it is rather like a taximeter in that, once it has become engaged in operations, and its engines started, it continues to use fuel whether or not it is active. The provision of more fuel and ammunition at the right moment, so that tanks are never immobilized for lack of either, is one of the most tricky aspects of commanding armor.

While CT(B) was refueling and reloading at the road junction, news was received from the air that Egyptian armor was advancing from the north. This was surprising. Presumably it must belong to the Gaza Division; but it seemed unlikely, and incompatible with normal Egyptian procedure, that the Gaza divisional commander would release his armor to take part in operations outside his area and with another division. Whether or not the news was accurate, those tanks from the north never materialized. But the risk that they might do so necessarily influenced Izzhak in his future movements. He left CT(A) behind at position 34 to counter the threat; and he ordered CT(B) to move forward as soon as it was refueled, to take positions 25 and 26 and make contact with the infantry at the road junction in position 12. It was now nine o'clock in the morning.

By this time CT(C), with its light tanks, had passed through the village of Rafa by way of the railway station and was continuing at speed in the direction of El Arish. Izzhak was with it. Shortly after noon they reached El Garadi, a few miles short of El Arish, where they met heavy artillery fire from the sand dunes between the road and the coast. The light tanks of CT(C) had no sooner mopped up these positions than fresh fire was encountered from the other side of the road, and reconnaissance showed that the positions were held in strength. The light tanks of CT(C) were now almost empty of fuel and had spent half their ammunition; so they were told to keep contact with the enemy and establish a "firm base" on the sand dunes astride the road, while CT(B), which had refueled and was some seven miles behind, was coming forward.

The attack by CT(B) could not be supported by artillery fire, since Izzhak's guns had been unable to keep pace with his armor. Support had to be provided from the air; two Meteors and two Ouragans delivered a "strike" at half past one in the afternoon, after which CT(B), which had made a wide detour from the road, went in against the southern flank of the positions, and took them for the loss of one tank and two half-tracks. There were 4 Archers and 12 57-mm. anti-tank guns in that position, and all were taken intact.

Leaving CT(C) to refuel, Izzhak ordered CT(B) to advance to the outskirts of El Arish, which it reached just before dark. Here it met heavy artillery fire and started to deploy. But night was falling, and Izzhak's brigade was now dispersed over a very wide area. He decided therefore that a pause for reorganization was necessary. Two companies in half-tracks were ordered to keep contact with the enemy, while the tanks of CT(B) were withdrawn some 5 miles back into Leaguer. At eight o'clock that night, they were joined by the other two combat teams and, two hours later, by the field artillery.

An hour before dawn, Izzhak was ready to continue. On the right, between the road and the coast, CT(C), whose AMXs with their wide tracks could best negotiate the sand dunes, was to advance straight into the outskirts of El Arish. In the center, CT(B) was to move astride the road until it reached the road junction at the entrance to the town. Here it was to split into two detachments, one going southward to mop up the military camps in that area, and the other pushing straight through the town and along the road to Qantara. On the left, CT(A) was to advance along an axis about a mile to the south of the road. Here there was thick sand—the same "impassable" sand which stretched southward for twenty-five miles to the northern edge of the Um Sheham positions—but the Super-Shermans, with which CT(A) was equipped, have very wide tracks which made them relatively speedy on this difficult going.

At dawn on D plus 4, air support was provided by Mustangs, who reported that there were 30 Sherman tanks in position between the brigade and El Arish. This seemed impossible; and when Izzhak asked for more details, the aircraft made a further reconnaissance which revealed that the vehicles were not tanks at all, but empty lorries that had been abandoned. For good measure it added the news that there were "hundreds of vehicles on their way from El Arish to Qantara." This meant that the enemy was in full retreat. The air force was turned on to it, and Izzhak ordered the (AMX) light tanks of CT(C) to hasten in pursuit.

At six-thirty that morning, Friday, D plus 4, the light tanks caught up with the tail of the enemy column. At that moment, the air strike was just over. The Egyptian crews, who had quitted their vehicles to take cover, were just scrambling back when the leading tanks of CT(C) came up. The result was devastation. Along the 120 miles between El Arish and Qantara, Israel took 385 Egyptian vehicles, of which 40 were Sherman tanks. Very few of them were actually hit, most of them being abandoned by their crews and left on the road, often with their engines still running. This was the effect of the air strike, although only three of the Sherman tanks were actually hit by aircraft.

In El Arish itself Israel took 27 more Shermans and 3 T.34s, mainly from the base workshops. In one camp a whole squadron of new tanks was found intact. Approximately 3000 prisoners were taken in this area, but thousands and thousands more padded away through the desert, and along the railway, with the blessings of Israel, who was not at all anxious to have to feed them.

The condition of El Arish when it was taken was fantastic. In one officers' mess the table was laid for a meal and the radio was still playing. In the bedrooms of Egyptian officers their clothing was still hanging in the closets, and photographs of their ladies were still on the dressing tables. A couple of Egyptian jeeps pulled up at a gasoline station in the town and asked to be refueled. An Israeli soldier started to serve his customers before he realized that they were all Egyptian officers.

All this was Friday evening. Does it throw any light on the question, still unanswered, of whether Nasser ever ordered a general withdrawal? In any event, the vast majority of his forces in that area were "successfully withdrawn" across the canal to Egypt, leaving behind them only their weapons, equipment, and vehicles, often their uniforms, which they buried in the sand, and invariably their boots, which littered the highway in thousands.

Meanwhile there remained only Gaza, defended by an entire Egyptian division, but completely sealed from all directions.

Eyeless in Gaza, Samson killed himself and his captors by pulling down those pillars. Gaza is one of the five old Philistine strongholds known to the Israelites in the days when its main traffic was in slaves and harlots, and its people worshiped heathen gods. Gaza was the scene of Maccabean fighting. Gaza lies on what used to be called the "Darab es Sultani," the royal road from Egypt to Baghdad. At Gaza, in the course of three separate attacks by British forces in 1917, the Turkish defenders inflicted 12,000 casualties.

The Gaza Strip is about 30 miles long and, in many places, not 4 miles wide. It is generally described as a finger pointing into Israel. When the armistice agreement was signed with Egypt in February 1949, she was left in occupation of this finger, which had never previously been Egyptian territory but was always part of Palestine. Under the United Nations' scheme of partition, agreed upon by Israel, but rejected by the Arab States, the Gaza Strip would have gone to the Arab part of the new state.

After the War of Independence, most of the refugees from southern Palestine assembled in the Gaza Strip, where they have since remained—one of the major problems of the Middle East. The blame for this problem must be shared by Israel; but blame for its protraction belongs almost exclusively to the Arabs. (This is discussed in Chapter XI.) In the Gaza Strip today there are 212,000 refugees, housed in camps which are not much better than the displaced-persons camps established after World War II for the remnant of European Jewry left by Hitler, and pervaded by a not dissimilar atmosphere of despair and lassitude.

The difference between the displaced-persons camps and those in the Gaza Strip is the difference between the Jewish and Arab temperaments. Whereas the Jews refused to accept their lot and resorted to the so-called "illegal immigration" to find a new home in Palestine, the Arabs have mostly achieved a kind of fatalistic content with conditions which offer them subsistence, on UNRWA rations and under UNRWA administration, without the need to work. While a number of Arabs have infiltrated into the refugee camps, preferring the camp conditions to those of their own homes in Egyptian territory, others who had any special skill or initiative have long disappeared from the Gaza Strip to find homes and employment elsewhere. What remains is largely human riff-raff, but nonetheless pathetic on that account.

Israel now had to take the Strip. But there were two very good reasons—the one military, and the other political and humane—for not launching a military attack on Gaza until this operation would be relatively bloodless. In the first place, the Gaza positions are topographically of immense strength—as the British learned, at a sore cost, during the First World War—and these same positions were now defended by an Egyptian division. And secondly, any prolonged and bloody battles might cause terrible casualties amongst the concentrated refugees, and the UNRWA administration who cared for them. Moreover, if the Strip could be sealed by the defenses of the kibbutzim which ringed its northern and eastern frontiers, and finally by the capture of Rafa in the south, Gaza itself, cut off from supplies from Egypt, would in due course be bound to surrender with little or no resistance.

The Egyptian defenses of the Gaza Strip—dominated by the Ali Muntar ridge, famous from the First World War—were well prepared with mutually supporting positions, mines, much barbed wire, and some concrete pill boxes, all sited for all-round defense. They were held by the Egyptian 8th Division, comprising only two brigades: a National Guard brigade deployed to the north of the wadi, and a Palestine brigade to the south in the neighborhood of Khan Yunis. Israel took the Gaza Strip as planned, with two battalions of the reserve brigade of NTF, supported by a detachment of armor.

Warning orders were issued to this force during the afternoon of D plus 3, after the fall of Rafa, and the operation order was received at two o'clock the following morning. Three hours later, the attack was made at dawn, the plan being to break into the position just north of the wadi, to cut the Strip in two, and to send forces simultaneously to the north and south. At this time there were available only the armor and one of the infantry battalions: one other infantry battalion was still reassembling from its antifedayeen deployment; and the third, which had been lent to Udah's brigade for its attack on Rafa, had not yet returned.

The assault on Gaza started with the armor's advancing straight down the road which runs due north into the town, east of the wadi. It was followed by infantry in lorries. The first position on the frontier, which was equipped with two anti-tank guns, resisted for thirty minutes. While it was being reduced, the brigade reconnaissance company captured a position directly opposite the ridge of Ali Muntar, and from there covered the lorried infantry which passed through and moved northeastward along the ridge, mopping up the Egyptian defenses and meeting little resistance, except from snipers.

By eight o'clock in the morning, the second battalion of this brigade, which had been deployed in more than thirty different detachments for its counter-fedayeen duties, had reassembled. It was put into buses and driven straight to the "battle," which it joined at the road junction 3 miles southwest of Gaza town. This junction, which is the tactical key to the whole Strip, had been taken, and was being held, by the armored detachment. An infantry company now took it over, while the remainder of the battalion followed in the wake of the armor which drove straight into the town. In the town itself there was at first no resistance.

By now the corps of UNRWA administrators in the town, and the UN observers belonging to the Mixed Armistice Commission, had persuaded the Egyptian commander to surrender before the civilian population, the refugees, or the UNRWA staff itself got seriously hurt; and a message was sent to the Israelis saying that the Egyptian commander was in the police station in the north-western section of the town, which had not yet been occupied. A few tanks and half-tracks were sent to pick him up but, on their journey, fire from bazookas and machine guns was opened on them, inflicting casualties and killing the company commander in the leading tank. The armor was then recalled and replaced by infantry, supported by tanks, with orders to mop up the town. By then resistance had ceased, and at noon a UN official got General Rajaani and drove him to brigade headquarters, where he signed an official surrender.

At two-thirty that afternoon the defenses from Gaza southward were taken by the brigade reconnaissance company followed by two infantry companies moving on foot along the ridge. Meanwhile the other infantry battalion was being relieved by an Israeli police force, under a military governor.

All that now remained was to mop up the southern half of the Gaza Strip, which included Khan Yunis, in which was 8th Divisional Headquarters. These concluding operations were not as bloodless as had been expected. The armor refueled itself in Gaza town, a process which took a long time on account of the traffic congestion; and it was not until midnight that it was ready to move south. In the early hours of the next day it ran into a road block comprised of anti-tank guns and mines, from which it lost two tanks and a half-track. But by two o'clock in the morning it had by-passed Khan Yunis. It reported, however, that the town of Khan Yunis was not yet clear.

Accordingly the armor was halted. The two infantry battalions were brought up, and an armored-car company was sent as reinforcement. Orders for a coordinated attack were issued at three o'clock in the morning, and by eight-thirty it was all over. The divisional commander, General Adouhi, whose headquarters were in Khan Yunis, signed an unconditional surrender.

One single Egyptian platoon refused to accept this order and by noon was still holding out against the Israeli armor. To avoid casualties, Mustangs attacked the position with rockets, the armor

An Egyptian at Gaza

driving in behind them. The northeastern sector of the Gaza Strip was mopped up by the "Home Guard"—members of the kibbutzim in the Yad Mordekhai area.

The Gaza Strip had been held by between 7000 and 8000 Egyptians. It was captured at the cost of 10 men killed. Not many Egyptians were killed on this occasion and no great number was taken prisoner. Many of them buried their weapons and uniforms in the sand and wandered back in their underclothes, 150 miles, to Egypt. Israel let them go. One pathetic group of Palestinian soldiers made a round trip. When they got to Egypt, they were turned back because they were not Egyptian, although they were serving in the

Egyptian Army; and in due course they returned disconsolately to the shelter of the prisoners' camp at Gaza.

The major problem was not capturing the Gaza Strip but controlling its civilian population. During the first day, until more police arrived, there was extensive looting of UNRWA stores. A curfew was imposed, but the Gaza Arabs sent out their women and children to continue the pilfering. In a few days the civilian administration was fairly effective, helped greatly by the fact that under the Egyptian administration everyone had an identity card which bore his photograph. This enabled fedayeen and ex-soldiers to be extracted from amongst the civilians.

The Strip continued to be administered under its existing laws. They were those of the former British administration, to which a couple of thousand Egyptian regulations had been added. These also were left in force, with the exception of a few which made it a laudable act to enter "Jewish-occupied Palestine" for felonious purposes. With the revocation of these laws, the collapse of Egypt's forces in Sinai was concluded.

IX

Seen from the Air

THE mystery of Egypt's failure to react in the air remains unresolved except on the basis that the Egyptians are incapable of quick reaction. If they knew in advance that the British and French intended to intervene by bombing their airfields, they were certainly better informed than Israel's air staff. The latter made their plans on the assumption that Egyptian airfields—once the Egyptians had opened this phase of the proceedings by bombing Israel's airfields—would have to be strenuously attacked by Israel's fighters, which would mean that Israeli ground forces would get no air support and must count on operating in conditions of Egyptian air superiority.

Apart from the military inconveniences of this condition, the Israeli Air Force was not disconcerted. It knew that Egypt's air strength comprised approximately 120 MIG 15s, 50 Ilyushin 28s (which are fighter bombers carrying a load of between two and three tons), 60 Vampires, and 20 Meteors. The fighters were based in the Suez Canal Zone and the bombers at Cairo West and Luxor.

Israel had reason to believe that only part of these aircraft could be made operational—perhaps only half the total number—since the Egyptian air crews and ground staff were not, as yet, very well trained or particularly efficient. Egyptian pilots had been met at various RAF courses in Britain. On each of two successive courses at Leaconfield, Yorkshire, which catered for a number of foreigners as well as RAF pilots, an Israeli had passed out top and taken the trophy, and the Egyptian student had come out bottom.

The enemy air force failed to react at all during the night of D-Day, after the paratroops had been dropped at Mitla and while they were being continually supplied by an "aerial railway," and during D plus 1 their aircraft failed to take the air until ten o'clock in the morning, and thereafter averaged less than one sortie per day from airfields which were less than 40 miles from their targets at the Monument. The total number of enemy sorties on D plus 1 was only about fifty, whereas four or five times that number had been anticipated; and on the following day the number was only doubled. All this was before there was any hint of Anglo-French intervention.

The operational inefficiency of the Egyptian Air Force remains unexplained. The MIGs never took the air in formations of less than four—and their formations were often of six or eight aircraft —which were successfully matched by Israel's fighters operating only in couples. The Egyptians made one or two adequate attacks which were pressed home against Israeli ground forces; but on the whole they were easily dissuaded and not very accurate. In air-to-air battles, it was found that a pair of Israeli fighters, operating at long range and short of fuel, was able to break off an engagement with six or eight MIGs. Only one Israeli fighter was ever pursued. And the only Israeli aircraft that was ever shot down in an air battle was a Piper Cub which was destroyed by a MIG after ten minutes of evasive action.

On both sides, casualties were relatively light, in view of the number of aircraft involved. Israel confirmed the destruction of 3 MIGs and 4 Vampires; she lost 1 Ouragan, 9 Mustangs, 2 Harvards and 3 Piper Cubs, all of which, with the exception of 1 Piper Cub, were destroyed or damaged by fire from the ground. Of these losses, 5 Mustangs and the Ouragan were able to be repaired and are now operational.

As I have said, only one aircraft, a Piper Cub, was shot down by Egyptian aircraft. The losses were mostly due, not to antiaircraft weapons, but to fire from small-arms by Egyptian infantry. It was surprising that these troops, who did not show great valor in ground-to-ground operations, were capable of organized defense against hostile aircraft. It needs more courage and discipline to let off with accuracy a rifle or automatic weapon against an aircraft which is strafing you than to sit in a well-dug and sandbagged gun emplacement shooting at enemy tanks or "thin-skinned" vehicles. One explanation is that the Mustang, which suffered the most from Egyptian fire, is particularly vulnerable on account of its unarmored radiator, which is situated underneath its engine.

From the viewpoint of the Israeli airmen, the quality of Egyptian pilots was not equal to that of the Egyptian infantry. This was suspected in advance. The Arab has no childhood background of "mechanical toys," and must start his military education from a basis of complete mechanical ignorance. This is less important—and of course more easily corrected—than the emotional aspects of his character. As everyone knows, the Arab is liable to collapse under any great emotional strain; and there are few emotional strains more severe than those of aerial warfare. What is more, the Arab is subject to black moods of depression which, under adversity, tend to render him useless. At RAF courses, if an Arab student failed to get a good report from one of his instructors, he usually relapsed into a fit, almost a trance, of utter dejection. These natural defects of character help to explain the accounts of aerial warfare that follow.

I can best describe the Israeli pilots by saying that the resemblance between the Israel Air Force and the RAF is no less marked than the resemblance between the Israeli and British Navies. This is intended not as a compliment but as an objective observation. During the two days that I spent at various air stations in Israel, going from one squadron to another, and being entertained at meals, I could not help remarking how the quiet, friendly, casual manner of speech, and the almost languid way in which a pilot would join our company and drop his flying kit into a corner, perfectly matched my recollections of visits to RAF stations and were so different from the cultivated "toughness" of my American memories. In Israel, nobody is "rarin' to go," but everyone is "willing to have a crack if it can't be helped." This is more strange because the Israeli temperament on the whole is less like the British than it is like the American, impetuous rather than indolent, and prone rather to vaunting its achievements than to taking them for granted.

After thirty-six hours spent mostly with the Israel Air Force, I happened to remark to a senior officer that it seemed to be composed exclusively of airmen who, although nearly all Sabras, came of European stock. Nobody said anything at the time, but a few hours later I was sitting at a squadron office and talking to a bunch of officers, when a squadron leader entered. He resembled so closely my neighbor in the Cotswolds—a farmer whose forebears had been connected with farming for many generations, and a young man whose war was spent in RAF air crews—that I had actually started to say, "Good heavens, Paul . . ." before I realized my mistake. It was not Paul, but a young man with the same gray eyes that always seemed focused on some point behind one's stomach. He was an Iraq Jew, coming from a family which could trace its descent for a thousand years in Iraq, and he commanded one of the crack squadrons in the Israel Air Force.

Danny said to me, "You can ask this chap whether or not the Orientals make good airmen."

It seemed to me that it would be an uncomfortable question, but it was answered without the least embarrassment by the Iraq squadron leader, who spoke good English and had understood Danny's suggestion. Actually he answered me in silence, with a slight gesture toward the other Air Force officers. I realized then that they were all Sabras but all of Oriental stock.

The aerial operations on D-Day, in connection with the parachute drop at Mitla, have been described in Chapter V. And in Chapter IV, I explained the "Yalu River rules" which prevented the Israel Air Force from taking any action except in response to Egyptian action and which meant in effect that they were compelled to pass the air initiative to Egypt.

On the following day, D plus 1, these rules were still in force, and no Israel aircraft was allowed to attack an Egyptian aircraft or to operate in support of Israel's ground forces until Egyptian aircraft had done so first. The release came (as described in Chapter V) when, after the capture of Thamed at six o'clock in the morning, Israeli troops were subjected to an attack by a pair of MIG fighters, and the paratroops at the Monument were severely punished by Meteors operating under a MIG escort. Not until these actions had been confirmed—in fact it was not until one o'clock in the afternoon of D plus 1—was the Israel Air Force let loose against ground targets. It was then allowed to attack the Egyptian forces which were being moved by transport into the Mitla area. During the remaining four hours of daylight, Israel's Air Force, operating at extreme range, flew more sorties in support of her ground forces than the Egyptian Air Force, operating close to its own airfields, flew during the whole of that day.

On the following day, which was D plus 2—with still no hint of Anglo-French intervention—the Israel Air Force threw everything it had onto the Egyptian ground forces. Yet on D plus 3 and D plus 4, Israel had a greater number of aircraft operational than when the campaign started. This was due not only to the competence of the maintenance staffs on Israel's airfields and to the excellent repair arrangements, but primarily to the fact that, from the point of view of the Air Force, the Sinai Campaign came at a most unfortunate moment. "We were caught on the wrong foot," the Air Force commander explained. He was educated in Britain and he served in the RAF throughout World War II. "We were halfway through the process of jet conversion." (This means, apparently, that the majority of pilots were being trained, and were still only half-trained, to fly jets instead of piston aircraft.) It was not till three days after the start of operations that Israel's Air Force was back on the right foot and at its maximum efficiency.

Once more, the conclusion is inescapable that if there was "collusion," and if collusion entailed advance preparation, the whole affair was conducted with an astonishing degree of incompetence that was quite incompatible with the efficiency of the actual operations.

During the campaign, the MIG 15 was discovered to have certain restrictions which proved to be serious handicaps. It has a range less than the Mystère. Its speed is structurally limited to "0.92 Mach," which means that it is less than supersonic, whereas the Mystère has no structural limitations. The MIG is unstable at certain speeds, it has no power controls for its elevators, and its 37-mm. cannon, which can fire at a rate of only 400 rounds per minute, is no match for the 30-mm. cannon of the Mystère, which fires at three times this rate.

The MIG has another technical disability which I must try to explain to other laymen like myself. It is related to a mysterious and malign influence known as G, which means the force of gravity. This G is something which an aircraft designer and a pilot have to combat. In the cockpit of the aircraft there is a dial which registers the extent to which G has exerted itself during the course of aerobatics. And after many dogfights many of Israel's fighter aircraft, whose tactics required them to make tight turns at maximum speeds, registered more than 8G, which means that they and their pilots had been subjected to eight times the force of gravity. This entails an enormous strain on everyone and everything. The gun sights become invisible. Limbs seem to be weighted with lead and are almost immovable. The most that a pilot can do is maneuver his plane with his feet on the rudder and his hands firmly on the "stick."

Therefore, in a well-designed fighter aircraft, all manual controls are operated from the "stick." In a MIG 15 the pilot has to move a hand from the "stick" in order to trim the aircraft. This severe disability is increased by the fact that, whereas most fighter aircraft are nowadays fitted with an arrangement which enables the pilot to wear an "anti-G" or pressurized flying suit, the MIG is not. Nor, for that matter, are the older types of fighter aircraft flown by the Israelis; so that it was not this particular disadvantage, or indeed any other technical factor, that made an Israeli pilot flying an obsolete British Meteor able to outfly an Egyptian in a MIG.

Aharon, who passed top out of a "Pilot Attack Instructors" (PAI) course at Leaconfield in Yorkshire, authorized me to reassure his former colleagues of the RAF that if they should ever be called upon to fly an obsolete Meteor aircraft, and they should happen to meet a MIG 15, they need not be unduly alarmed. At low altitudes the Meteor can make tight turns which the MIG cannot follow; and if it attempts to do so, the effect of its swept wings is that it loses speed and is no longer a superior aircraft. The remedy for the MIG is to dive to recover speed—there is no other way of doing so for any jet aircraft—and if the encounter takes place at low altitude the MIG is unable to dive without hitting the earth.

Aharon suggests that I warn any RAF Meteor pilots that the lever which releases his wing tanks—a necessary preliminary to combat—must be pulled right back. (I am referring to something called the "Emergency Carrier Release.") There is a tendency to pull it only halfway, in which case only one wing tank will fall off. One Israel Meteor whose pilot made this mistake found himself doing a complete roll at less than 2000 feet. This, I gather, is dangerous.

More modern than the Meteor, but also obsolete, the Ouragan proved to be an adequate match for a MIG in air combat. Ladia, a flight commander, told me, "On D plus two at eleven-fifty hours I went out with my number two to give ground support to the paratroops at Mitla. We were flying Ouragans, each armed with eight rockets and two napalm bombs, as well as our four twenty-millimeter cannons. When we got over Gaza I found that I could not transfer fuel from my wing tanks to my main tanks, which meant that, if I went as far as Mitla, I should not be able to remain long over the area without running out of fuel. So I notified Control and asked for a closer target. I was told to wait, but at that same time I heard on my radio another pair telling Control that they had seen an armored convoy of fifty tanks moving from Bir Hama eastward." (This was almost certainly the message which proved to be inaccurate and, when intercepted by Benyameen's armored brigade, caused the latter to make the dispositions recounted in Chapter VII. The tanks were in fact much farther to the west, moving eastward from Bir Gifgafa, not Bir Hama.)

Ladia still speaking: "Ground Control called me and gave me permission to look for that convoy. At that time I was above Bir Hama flying southward. I gave an order for a turnabout and started searching eastward without watching the sky. I was starting to go down from eight thousand feet, when I heard a shout from my number two: 'Break—MIGs on your tail!' I broke left and saw that my number two had three MIGs on his own tail. I warned him and told him to break harder, and he answered that he was going to jettison his bombs and his wing tanks. I did the same. I noticed that tracers were passing close to my wing and I broke harder myself.

"My number two shouted, 'Break right and not left!' I broke right and saw a MIG followed by my number two and two MIGs following him—everybody shooting. When I broke right there was a MIG on my wing breaking left. We crisscrossed each other several times, passing each other at about ten meters. After this, because I was slower, I found myself on the MIG's tail and when he saw that he was losing he started to pull away, and I was in a good position for firing.

"As I was about to fire, I saw tracers coming from behind on both sides of me. I looked in my mirror and saw a MIG filling it. We were at three thousand feet. I did a 'split S'—a wing turn toward the ground—hoping that the MIG would follow me and crash. I had difficulty in pulling out myself, but unfortunately the MIG stayed upstairs.

"Then my number two shouted again, 'Break—there's three more behind you,' and again I saw tracers. I flew very low, throwing my plane all over the place to try and avoid the MIGs. I looked right and left and in the mirror, but could see no MIGs, so I straightened the plane and started to fly level and very low. Then I saw more tracers coming from behind. As I broke away, I heard the voice of my best friend coming over my radio. He was up there with a pair of Mystère fighters and he took on the MIGs and shot down one of them a little later.

"I started going home, but found I had no fuel on the clock, so I had to make a forced landing in the desert—without incident. Within twenty minutes a Piper Cub came and took me away. We salvaged the aircraft, which was flying again by the next day. When I got home, I learned that my number two had been hit by two thirty-seven-millimeter cannon shots, but he got back all right. They told us that we had been fighting with eight MIGs and that there were four more giving cover up above."

Yankle, who passed top out of the RAF course following the one at which Aharon had done the same, told me, "On D plus two at noon we took off with a pair of Ouragans against tank convoys near Bir Gifgafa. We were each loaded with two napalm bombs. We were flying at thirteen thousand five hundred feet above Gebel Libni, when my number two told me that two aircraft were passing above us in the opposite direction. We were flying abreast, my number two and I, five hundred yards apart, each watching the other's tail.

"Half a minute later I saw an aircraft on my number two's tail, but I wasn't sure if it was a MIG or a Mystère—though I thought a MIG. I told him to break left and jettison his bombs and wing tanks. I did the same.

"What the MIG ought to have done was to make a pass and gain height and try again. But instead, he came into a turn with my number two. His radius of turn was much bigger than the Ouragan's, and when I followed him in his turn, I started to close. My number two couldn't release his wing tanks, but in spite of this the MIG couldn't close the turn.

"I saw the MIG shooting in the turn and of course missing because of the very high angle-off [deflection] and because of the high G. I made the same mistake myself—I fired one short burst in the turn and missed. I knew of course that there was another MIG somewhere above, but I couldn't see it. I was anxious about it. Anyway, I could see that the first MIG was closing the turn on my number two, and if he changed the bank it would save him, so I told him to do so. Then I saw some more MIGs up above.

"This change of direction brought me into a favorable position to fire on the first MIG, and I gave him a long burst and saw pieces fall off him. He immediately pulled up and straightened his wings. I shot at him again, hit him again, and saw a big hole in his left wing and something burning and a lot of white smoke. I shot again but only one cannon fired, but it hit him near his jet pipe. After that, there was black smoke coming out of his jet pipe. Because my cannons were not working any more, I then came home." The destruction of that MIG fighter was later confirmed.

Jack, who commands a Mystère squadron, took part in the "first world première" of a Mystère in battle. He was on patrol with his number two when he got word from the ground that troops were being attacked by four Egyptian Vampires. Without bothering to jettison either their wing tanks or their rockets, the two Mystères shot down all four Vampires in less than two minutes.

Later that same day, on another sortie, he was on a ground-support mission and flying at 20,000 feet when he saw two MIGs below him flying in the opposite direction. He and his number two went to engage them.

Jack said, "The MIGs broke and got separated. One of them went home. My number two was in a favorable position to shoot, but, on account of his turn, it was at a high angle-off. Since I was in an even more favorable position, I told my number two to break and I closed in. The MIG pilot made a mistake which a lot of them seemed to make, because they had been told how wonderful the MIG is. They think they can get away by changing direction with full power and making a climbing turn. They can't do this, because although the MIG can climb faster, the higher speed of the Mystère when it starts to climb cancels it out.

"I didn't lose at all on the climb and I was able to cut in and close to two hundred fifty yards. I opened fire—a fairly short burst—and saw the MIG go into a very fast spin. I followed him down about eight thousand feet and saw him straighten out of the spin and use his ejector seat. Unfortunately his parachute didn't open. The MIG went into a great blaze before it hit the ground." A few of the fragments from this aircraft were subsequently collected for examination.

During a pleasant evening that I spent in his home, the commander of Israel's Air Force summed up the operations. He said that, in the event of attacks on targets in Israel by Egyptian aircraft, his plan had been to hit the Egyptian Air Force with everything that he had. But when on D plus 1 the Egyptians had not attacked targets in Israel, but were strafing her ground forces instead, he put all available aircraft on to support missions.

His technical conclusions were something of a mixed bag. The T.34 tank can be knocked out by a 20-mm. cannon with a hit on either the spare fuel tanks or the bogies. The Ouragan was a much better airplane than had been thought. It is extremely reliable: it suffered from no technical failures in the four days of fighting, despite many hits; and one Ouragan which had a 37-mm. shell that passed through the main spar and entered the fuel tank got safely back to base. It is a magnificent gun platform, much steadier than the Mystère; and it is more maneuverable than the MIG and better than the Venom. (His comparison might be colored, I thought, by the fact that the Air Force had had its first Mystère fighter only nine months previously, and might have flown them to even better advantage with a little more experience.) So far as the timing of the campaign was concerned, the Air Force would have been much better pleased if it had been postponed for six months, until the spring of next year. By then, both pilots and ground staff would have completed their "conversion" from piston aircraft to jets.

The first intimation given to the commander of Israel's Air Force that any operations were contemplated was at two o'clock in the morning of Thursday, October 25. The previous day he had been conducting some seventy important visitors from the United States around an airfield. As he watched the aircraft giving a display, he never imagined that four days later they would be engaged in operations.

Whereas the primary task of any air force is normally to engage, and neutralize or destroy, the enemy's air force, the task given to Israel's Air Force on this occasion was "to support the ground forces and to be prepared to counter enemy interference." This was a role for which it had never planned. All previous planning had been based on an appreciation that it would take six days to reduce the Egyptian Air Force, of which the first three days would be critical. It was never believed that the numerical superiority of Egypt would be decisive, since the key to air victory lies, not in numbers, but in pilot efficiency and in ground organization and maintenance. In the view of Israel's Air Force commander, the fighter efficiency of his air force depends ninety per cent on preparation in peacetime.

This was the doctrine that enabled Israel to put such a large number of aircraft into the air from the very beginning of operations. The Flying School was closed down immediately. All the instructors had operational or observer jobs, and the school itself was ready to provide a number of operational units in the space of six hours.

It is difficult to appreciate the extraordinary efficiency of the maintenance staff. It had to be efficient. In a country like Israel there is no "pipeline" of supply bringing fresh aircraft from the factory. The war has to be won with the aircraft that are in the country. Everything, therefore, depends on repair and maintenance. For example, every single Mustang that was able to struggle back to its base, no matter how badly damaged, was mended and back in the air in twenty-four hours or less.

Certain conclusions are inescapable. If Egypt had had air superiority over the battlefield—as was anticipated by the General Staff—the Sinai Campaign would still have been won. If there had been no Anglo-French intervention, Israel's Air Force might have been preoccupied with Egyptian airfields and so could have given less support to her ground forces. There is no doubt that the degree of support which she was able to accord saved Israel's Army from several additional days of fighting and, in consequence, it saved casualties. This was the Sinai Campaign seen from the air. The view was impressive.

X

Sea View

ALL navies are traditionally courteous to their guests, and their courtesy is often practiced with a touch of grave humor. Humor is never allowed to disturb the dignity of an occasion; everybody's face is suitably solemn; and the joke is the more pleasant on that account. Nobody smiled while I was piped aboard the *Hunt* class destroyer recently known as the *Ibrahim-El-Awal,* formerly H.M.S. *Cottesmore.* I could not salute, because I wasn't in uniform; I could not take off my hat, because I wasn't wearing one. The sentry presented arms, and I stood approximately to attention.

I had last seen this ship when she was one of our escorts in the Sicilian assaults of 1943. Before that, she had helped to take us on a commando raid to Norway. Since her war career with the British Navy, she had led a cosmopolitan life. For a while she was lent to one of the Chinese governments. Later she was returned to Britain and sold to Egypt. And on October 30, 1956, she was captured at sea by the Israel Navy and towed into port. The Israeli destroyer which boarded her and took her in tow had also been purchased from Britain. She was once commanded by my brother-in-law. It is this kind of coincidence through the looking-glass which helps to make Israel an exciting country.

The Israel Navy is composed only of destroyers, frigates, and smaller vessels such as motor torpedo boats (MTBs), motor launches (MLs) and various landing craft. By the world's naval standards, it is of course a diminutive navy; but by any standards it is an efficient and proud service. The time that I spent in its company was strangely, nostalgically familiar. The quiet manner of speech, the dry humor, that particular kind of aloofness or detachment in the course of recollection, the impeccable manners of everyone, the smartness of naval ratings when we boarded, or departed from, a ship, and the competence with which a launch was manned and handled—I might have been right back some fifteen years, perhaps in Scapa Flow. The only obvious difference between the Navy at Haifa and the Navy at Scapa, the Clyde, Plymouth, or Portsmouth, was that at Haifa the naval officers spoke English with a slightly foreign accent.

I am very ignorant of naval affairs and have always been strictly what the Royal Navy describes as a "pongo" and the RAF used to describe as a "brown type stooging about at low altitudes." Nevertheless, during my years in one department or another of Combined Operations, I spent a large part of my time with both the British and American Navies, sometimes living for weeks on end in seaborne quarters. In my professional dealings with sailors, I have often been infuriated, but always enchanted. And while I cannot say that I love the sea, because it tends to make me seasick, I have the deepest affection for warships and the people who serve them.

I am not trying to say that the navies of various countries are very much alike. I could never find anything in common between the British and American Navies, except that they were both doing similar jobs. But while the Israel Army has a character quite different from any other that I have ever known, the Israel Navy and Air Force are both cut to something very like the British pattern.

The commander in chief of Israel's Navy explained to me, when I first got to his headquarters, that he had three tasks: the protection of Israel's sea lanes; the protection of Israel's coasts and centers of production—the latter being all situated near the coast; and the provision of support for the Army.

In planning to carry out these tasks, Israel had always been in a state of technical inferiority vis-à-vis her main enemy, Egypt.

Her attempts to reach naval parity with Egypt can be seen in two phases. During the period 1949-1950, immediately after the War of Independence, Egypt had two *Hunt* class destroyers (formerly H.M. Ships *Cottesmore* and *Atherstone*), three frigates, and one sloop, all bought from Britain. This was the force which Israel tried to match by various purchases during the ensuing years.

Then came the second period of 1955-1956, when Britain sold to both Israel and Egypt two Z class destroyers apiece, and Egypt made relatively massive purchases from Russia, Czechoslovakia, and Yugoslavia. By October 1956, Egypt had actually received 2 "Skouri" destroyers from behind the Iron Curtain, the 2 Z class destroyers and the 2 *Hunt* class destroyers which have been previously mentioned, 4 armed mine layers (with more on order), and something like 20 MTBs. She also had a program for receiving Iron Curtain submarines. This gave her a very substantial degree of technical superiority over Israel.

Whereas technical superiority proved to be of no value to the Egyptian Army, it is taken much more seriously in the case of naval armaments. There ought to be a parallel between armored and naval warfare. In each case the factors are speed, maneuverability, armor, and the range and caliber of armaments. If either a tank or a warship of one side can fire a heavier shell at a longer range than its opponent on the other side, it ought to come out best. As we have seen, Israel's exponents of tank warfare found ways of offsetting the superiority of new Russian and Czech equipment over American and French Shermans. But all naval experts seem to assume—no doubt with experience and good reason—that a warship which has a speed equal to that of its enemy, and a gun with a longer range, ought always to win. It can keep up with its antagonist and, while remaining outside the range of her guns, continue to shoot at her until she is sunk.

This simple formula depends on the relative states of training of the two parties. In the case of armor, it was clear that the Egyptians were not sufficiently susceptible to training to be able to handle their new and modern weapons. This does not seem to be quite true of the Egyptian Navy, and the extensive training program which her officers and crew had undergone in Poland and Russia, as well as in Britain, seemed to have been more effective than the training by Russian and German instructors and technicians given to her soldiers. The Israel Navy considers that the simple fact that Egypt had been able to get all her warships fully operational in so short a time after taking delivery proved that the training had not been ineffective.

Egypt's warships were all at sea during the period of the Sinai Campaign. Even the unfortunate *Ibrahim–El–Awal* (*née Cottesmore*) fought bravely, and not incompetently—except in one vital respect—until she was finally crippled by much stronger Israeli forces. Accordingly, while the Israel Navy views without alarm the technical superiority of Egypt, she regards her enemy more seriously, and takes fewer risks and more precautions, than does the Israel Army. I think this a characteristic of most navies, and certainly of the Royal Navy of Britain. It seems very reasonable. While a military mistake may mean a battle lost, a naval mistake will more often mean national disaster; and while each individual military task may be very important, there are few naval tasks which are not vital.

During the period of the Sinai Campaign, Israel's Navy executed her three tasks with complete success. The Merchant Navy was taken under immediate control, and all ships proceeded to and from Haifa without interruption. The sea lanes were kept clear. The coast and centers of production were duly protected and were not subjected to any attack from the sea, except for the few rounds fired by the *Ibrahim–El–Awal* before she was engaged and captured. But there was no major opportunity of undertaking the third task—that of supporting the Army.

This was a pity. Israel's landing-craft establishment is obviously most efficient; and it still seems to me, as an old devotee of amphibious warfare, that there would have been a lovely chance of landing a force somewhere to the west of El Arish to cut the enemy's communications along the northern road. This operation was not undertaken and, as it happened, those communications were adequately cut by air action.

Nor did the MTBs succeed in making contact with the Egyptian Navy, which—with the exception of the *Ibrahim–El–Awal,* and of two unfortunate frigates which got sunk in the Red Sea by the British—never went far from Port Said and Alexandria. This was a sad disappointment for the MTB squadron. It is obviously a force of superb efficiency and spirit. Moreover it was one hundred per cent operational, which is rare for such craft and is a tribute to the very efficient maintenance and repair installations at Haifa. Nevertheless, although the MTB patrols made frequent contact with strange ships at sea, they all proved to be neutral.

This problem of a mass of neutral ships milling about a small expanse of sea was something new in naval warfare. British and French ships were all over the place. The Americans were the worst offenders, and kept on popping up on the radar screen with formidable squadrons at unexpected moments. It was really rather remarkable that nobody shot anyone by accident.

American "intervention" played no small part in the affair of *Ibrahim–El–Awal.* This ship was allowed to approach to within five miles of Israel's coast, and to open fire on Haifa, in the belief that she was one of the American ships whose arrival, at some unstated time, was expected. They were to embark what were called, in the European newspapers, the "American refugees" escaping from the disaster that was imminent in Israel. And these American vessels were quite a feature of the naval engagement described to me by the commander of the Israel forces which captured the *Ibrahim–El–Awal* that morning.

A man of medium height and well proportioned, the commander has a soft voice and a sardonic humor. A type exactly the opposite to Udah, the brigade commander in the north who is described in Chapter VIII, he can make the same boast that he has "come up the hard way" and that, at the age of fourteen, he was already at work. While Udah was delivering the milk, Menachem (as we will call him) was working as a builder's laborer. Sitting in his cabin in a Z class ex-British destroyer, he offered me British gin or British whisky while, relaxed, modest, and courteous, he told me the story in a series of understatements.

Menachem's squadron was some 40 miles at sea when, at about three o'clock in the morning, it was reported to him that Haifa was being bombarded. At this time there was nothing to be seen on his radar screens, but he was informed that the ship which had opened fire was withdrawing at high speed on a zig-zag course westward. This seemed a reasonable action for any enemy vessel to take, with the intention of turning later either southwestward for Port Said or northeastward for Beirut. At that time, in the darkness, the Israel commander had no means of knowing what kind of force he had against him or what it was up to. The truth was too implausible even to be suspected. Surely a single warship would not venture to within 5 miles of Haifa simply in order to open fire, do no damage whatsoever, and run away again into an area patrolled and controlled by Israel's naval forces? It seemed more likely that this ship was part of a larger force and part of a trap to lead Israel's warships into an engagement with much superior forces.

Menachem had with him two Z class destroyers and a frigate. It was possible that he might find himself lured into action with four destroyers or more, two of them being "Skouris" with a greater range, greater speed, and heavier armament than his own. He decided to move at top speed on a course slightly west of north. It proved a fortunate choice.

At this moment Menachem's suspicions of a trap were reinforced by the simultaneous appearance on his radar screens of a single ship about 20 miles to the northeastward, and a squadron of four ships to the northwestward. But the matter was still in doubt, on account of the American "rescue forces" which were on their way to Haifa. Accordingly, Menachem signaled to the squadron, asking them, "WHAT SHIP?" The squadron replied that it was American, and after a few flickering exchanges Menachem felt confident that these were in fact the American ships whose arrival was expected. But his simultaneous communications to starboard were more exciting. When the single ship was asked her identity, the question was repeated, and in a faltering style which suggested Egyptian calligraphy on a signaling lamp.

Two ships cannot continue indefinitely to ask each other who they are. If neither of them will answer the question, a state of mutual hostility is assumed. And at this moment came the start of morning dusk and the first sight of a silhouette with the backward-sloping mast which is characteristic of the *Hunt* class destroyers. Therefore Menachem signaled to the Americans, "AM OPENING FIRE ON ENEMY SHIP PLEASE KEEP AWAY." With a brief acknowledgment the Americans altered course and obliged.

Thus began the engagement of the Israeli squadron with what turned out to be the *Ibrahim–El–Awal*. The Egyptian ship was firing efficiently, her first salvo falling short of the Israeli ships, and her second salvo passing over them, so that she had got her "bracket" on her enemy. The Israeli commander altered course slightly to the westward, so that, by drawing away from the Egyptian ship, he could take advantage of his superior range and speed. He could now punish the Egyptian ship, while the latter was unable to hit back since all her shots fell short.

An Israeli Dakota now joined the engagement and asked the Israeli commander how it could help. The latter replied that it could best help by keeping out of the zone of his gunfire, and shortly afterward the airplane flew homeward. Later it led to the scene a couple of Ouragans who made an effective contribution; and shortly afterward an MTB flotilla arrived, but was directed to keep out of it. The engagement continued satisfactorily, with the Israeli ships untouched, and the Egyptian destroyer taking punishment until, suddenly, she was seen to make a turn of 180 degrees and to stop. It was then observed that a white flag was flying from her mast and that her crew were jumping overboard and taking to the rafts.

The normal procedure would be to pick up survivors and sink

the enemy destroyer with a torpedo. The hazards of attempting to board her and tow her some 60 miles back to Haifa were very great. Attacks by superior forces of ships and aircraft were possible at any moment. And it was a century or so since naval warfare had been of a kind that allowed a warship to be taken alive and brought back to port. But the prize was very tempting, and Menachem decided to go after it. He ordered his sister ship to take up station on the port side of the enemy, and to land a boarding party prepared to take her in tow. At the same time, he set about picking up survivors himself and ordered his MTB flotilla to take the Egyptian wounded at full speed back to port.

Normally when a ship is taken in tow she casts a tow overboard herself and it is picked up by the rescuing ship or tug. In this case, the tow rope, which is exceedingly heavy, had to be hoisted aboard the *Ibrahim* by the small boarding party, who enlisted, for this purpose, those members of the Egyptian crew who had not already disembarked.

It was an anxious time. The whole party were more or less opposite Beirut, which is, of course, Arab territory and hostile. The Egyptian destroyer was crippled; she had no steam in her boilers; her electricity was gone; she would not answer to her helm; she had taken in a lot of water; her pumps were not working, and the Egyptians had attempted to scuttle her. They had failed to do so, mainly because one of the cocks was so rusty that nobody had been able to open it. When the process of towing began, *Ibrahim–El–Awal* swung wildly from side to side and progress toward Haifa was scarcely perceptible.

The Israel boarding party comprised "one of everything"—one electrician, one engineer, one signal man, and so on. Its commander persuaded the Egyptian captain, who was still on board, to take him on a tour of the ship. The cocks were quickly closed to arrest the scuttling process; the pumps were got working; the fires were got under control, and the intake of water from the various holes was arrested. Soon the rudder was sufficiently repaired for the ship to answer to her helm.

Meanwhile a fire-fighting ship and a tug were on their way from Haifa, while ambulances were waiting in port to rush the wounded Egyptians to hospital. The fire-fighting ship went alongside and added her pumps to those aboard; but the tug, when she got to the scene, was too slow to be of use. Indeed, by this time, the Israeli destroyer was towing her prize at such a speed that the tug could scarcely keep up. Israel's fighter aircraft were now overhead and the *Ibrahim-El-Awal* was towed back to the port which, five hours earlier, she had been attempting to bombard.

When the Egyptian ship had been got into dry-dock, some strange things were found about her. Although she had fought her guns quite bravely, no attempt had been made to repair or control the damage. In all navies there is a meticulous drill by which damage from enemy gunfire which causes leaks, or which starts a conflagration, is brought under control. This had not been practiced. No attempt had been made to stem the inflow of water in various places where the ship had been holed. Nobody had thought of using any of the wooden pegs or wedges of various sizes that a warship carries with her for such occasions. A fire had started in the paint locker, just aft of a 40-mm. anti-aircraft gun which had received a direct hit and had blown up. The paint locker had contained several tins of paint which had been opened and half used. No warship in its senses would deliberately go into action in this state, since the paint fumes could easily catch fire—as in fact they did.

Nor had any attempt been made to attend to casualties. The sick bay had not been manned. And although the engagement had continued as a running fight for one hour and twenty minutes, and there were 4 killed and 18 wounded out of a crew of 153, not one of them had received even a first-aid dressing. They had simply been left on deck.

There is doubt and dispute about the way in which the ship was finally crippled. It is quite clear that something caused her steering to go out of action, but not clear what it was. The Ouragan had put a rocket through the wardroom, which had severed all the electrical wires passing from bow to stern, and this would have disconnected the rudder from the wheel. But you can steer a ship without electrical power in an emergency, and it seemed that no one had tried to do so. This might have been due to the fact that it would have been pointless, anyway, since the boilers had lost steam.

It is quite interesting to see how this happened. Apparently a warship has two of everything, so that if one is broken or knocked out of action, there is a substitute. She has two boilers and two fuel tanks; and normally one boiler is connected to each of the tanks, so that if one tank is damaged, only one boiler is put out of action. The *Ibrahim–El–Awal* went deliberately into action with both her boilers connected to the port-side fuel tank; so that when a near miss fell close alongside and exploded under water, causing a leak in this tank and letting sea water get mixed with fuel oil, *both* boilers lost steam, and the ship stopped.

This is, of course, a layman's description of what happened, and it is pieced together by conversations with many of the people who took part in it. Doubtless it contains some nautical absurdities in its phraseology; but even if this makes the sailors laugh, it may make the story more comprehensible to others.

The pilot of one of the Ouragans which had attacked the *Ibrahim* told me his story:

"We were ordered to arm two Ouragans with sixteen armor-piercing rockets each. We took off at six hundred hours and went in search of the Egyptian ship. There were a great many ships in the sea at that time. When we got near the area, Ground Control directed us to a ship which I was about to attack when it seemed to me that it was a merchant ship. I reported this to Ground Control, but Control ordered me to attack it. Three times I reported that it was a merchant ship, and three times Ground Control said that it was the *Ibrahim*. Then a Dakota came and pin-pointed the target for us.

"The weather was cloudy, and we were flying at five thousand feet. The wake of the ship showed that she had been turning from west to due east, but at the time of our attack she was on a course of one hundred twenty degrees [southeast]. I attacked out of the sun and made my run along the ship from bow to stern.

"I dived and released all sixteen rockets, at about five hundred yards from a height of seven hundred feet. I broke from the ship before I could see the hits, but I saw pieces of metal in the air. I broke high and to the left and saw my number two [the second Ouragan] leaving the ship after releasing his rockets. After this attack by my number two, the ship was hidden in smoke. There were two kinds of smoke, some black and some very white.

"All this time the Dakota was watching. As we left the ship it sent us a message that we had scored a good hit and that the ship was slowing down. A little later we heard that the ship had surrendered. We never saw any anti-aircraft fire coming from the ship." (In fact all anti-aircraft guns were firing during the attack.)

Meanwhile, the story had got around Israel that the crew of the *Ibrahim-El-Awal* had been set free and sent back to Egypt to fetch a second destroyer—"this time a 'Skouri.'"

By the time I saw *Ibrahim*, which was Thursday, November 15, a fortnight after the action, the damage was nearly repaired; there was steam in her boilers, and she was about to start her trials before going into service with the Israel Navy. An accurate tally of the damage made by the port engineers was: 4 direct hits, including 1 on the bows which blew up an anti-aircraft gun and ignited the paint locker; 1 hit from an armor-piercing rocket from the air, which had entered the ship on the starboard side; over 70 holes from splinters on the port side; the port-side fuel tank pierced below the water line.

It is bad luck for so many navies that, while their task is vital, it is so rarely spectacular. Although Israel's MTBs kept constant patrols in enemy waters, they never had a chance of a target. And although Menachem's squadron was almost continuously at sea, it had nothing but the *Ibrahim-El-Awal* to shoot at.

On one other occasion, Menachem had cause for excitement.

He was patrolling off Gaza, before the capture of the Strip, when a squadron of ships appeared on his radar screens. He made a signal asking for their identity. Possibly the yeoman was not on deck at the time and the inexpert style of the reply led him to hope that these were Egyptians and this was another chance of engagement.

He was soon to be disillusioned. When he repeated his question a competent signalman replied that, once more, it was an American squadron. The squadron was heading toward the shore, and when Menachem asked it where it was going, it replied, "I don't know for sure." In fact it was trying to find Gaza in order to evacuate some of the staffs of the UN and UNRWA.

There were only two other occasions on which the Navy was able to take a positive part in the campaign. The first has already been described in Chapter VI, when a flotilla of landing craft was got to the Gulf of Aqaba to join in the operations against Sharm el Sheikh. The other incident was a case of salvage; and the object salvaged was a MIG fighter.

This fighter had been severely damaged in an air battle and was unable to get back across the canal. It had force-landed in a lagoon about 60 miles east of the canal and close by a small Arab fishing village. Here it lay partly submerged until discovered by air reconnaissance. There was no chance to recover it by land, and the Navy was asked to do it.

The job was undertaken by a medium-sized landing craft (LCM), accompanied by one of the larger types of infantry landing craft (LCI). These two craft were escorted to the entrance of the lagoon, which is only 20 yards wide and extremely difficult to navigate, owing to a very swift current.

In the entrance, and in the lagoon itself, there was nowhere more than two and a half fathoms of water; and the MIG itself lay in a half-fathom. The LCM managed to get into the lagoon against the current, but could not then reach the MIG.

By this time an officer had landed from a Piper Cub and "captured" the Arab village, whose inhabitants were enlisted to help salvage the aircraft. There were also a small launch and three fishing boats, all of which were now brought into service. The launch belonged to an Egyptian contractor whose practice it was to use it for fishing during the annual three-month season. The season had closed by the end of October, and the foreman in charge was exceedingly worried at the thought of what his master would say when told of the improper use to which his launch was put. The foreman was appeased by a gift of Israeli rations, with which the villagers also were paid for their services, and everyone became cooperative.

The launch could get to the MIG but could not dislodge it until a Dakota had been summoned and had dropped air bags, one of which was fastened under each wing, so that the aircraft could be floated. Once afloat, the MIG was towed to the entrance of the lagoon by the motor launch and the three fishing boats. Since their course lay dead against wind, sail could not be used, and the fishing boats had to be poled through the water by the many willing workers. It was a cheerful but protracted process, and it took thirty-six hours to get the MIG to the entrance of the lagoon. In order to get the tow through the entrance, it was mounted on three kapok life rafts from the LCI, after which it was pulled out by the launch, with the LCM standing by to help if necessary.

By now a merchant ship had been summoned from Haifa. She drew 18 feet, and there was very little water under her keel when she hoisted the MIG aboard before returning to port. This operation—a combined operation in several senses—took seven days to complete. On an Israeli air station I later inspected the MIG.

Thus the Navy repaid in kind the assistance given by the Air Force in the *Ibrahim–El–Awal* engagement. It was a happy transaction.

XI

What Prospects?

HAS anything at all been gained, either by Israel or by the world, from this remarkable campaign? Some people say that nothing is ever achieved by war. Historically it would be easier to prove that nothing is ever achieved without war. It has always taken a war to upset a dictator—Napoleon, Hitler, Mussolini. Nasser has never pretended that he is anything but a dictator, nor has he failed to declare in categorical terms (*The Philosophy of the Revolution*) the scope of his ambitions, which are no less aggressive than those of his Nazi and Fascist predecessors. By the Sinai Campaign he has undoubtedly been checked, both through the loss of half his Army, and through the damage to his prestige. And even if his prestige has been handsomely repaired by the United States, his Arab neighbors—none of whom have ever loved him very dearly—will have observed some discrepancy between his martial threats and boastful declarations before the campaign (and even during it) and the conduct of his soldiers on the battlefield.

Today there is not much left of the Egyptian Army. It is true that a large proportion of its men, and a still larger proportion of its officers, padded their way back to Egypt, where they were greeted as heroes by Nasser, extensively decorated, and carefully isolated from the public—lest they tell the truth of what had befallen them—and that these men can very easily be re-armed. It is true, also, that the arms and equipment lost on the battlefield are being replaced by Russia. But an army which has been routed in this manner has "learned in its heart"—to use Dayan's phrase—that it cannot defeat Israel by force of arms; and the other Arab states have learned it also. To this extent the objects of the campaign have been achieved.

There have of course been other concrete gains for Israel: relief from the imminent threat of invasion; relief from the fedayeen raids that were launched from Gaza (although Egypt has continued to mount her fedayeen activities from Jordan); and relief from the blockade in the Gulf of Aqaba. Otherwise, the principal gain has been a little breathing space.

What is to be done with that breathing space? Obviously it ought to be used for the negotiation of peace. This is the only thing that Israel wants. If she had been left to herself, she would have won her right to peace negotiations by her military victory; she could get it no other way; she had been seeking it by other ways for the seven years that followed her armistice agreements in 1949. And now it is the UN which has prevented peace negotiations between Israel and Egypt from being forced upon the latter. A strange use to which the UN has put itself!

The Arabs cannot negotiate with Israel, because they cannot recognize Israel's existence. You can say to an Arab, "Look! We agree that you *can* argue that there ought never to have been an Israel. Nevertheless there *is* an Israel, and she has nearly two million citizens. So let us start arguing from that indubitable fact." But the Arab will only reply, "There never should have been an Israel; and we do not recognize that there is; and the only possible argument is how and when Israel can be liquidated."

The viewpoint of the Arabs is that Israel does not exist; the viewpoint of the world is that Israel does exist. How can these two contradictory viewpoints be in any way reconciled and brought into the focus of a peace settlement? It is this question that I have to try to answer at the end of this chapter. It means that the Sinai Campaign has to be seen in the context of the future and the past.

And we had better look back first, before trying to look forward. For the sake of continuity I shall have to repeat a few of the facts that have already been mentioned in Chapter II.

On October 25, 1956, when Israel mobilized her Army, a state of war had long existed between herself and her neighbors. It was modern war, or the new-type war, in which you can defeat an enemy more surely by all sorts of other means than by orthodox military operations. These were to come later, and not very much later. In the meantime, while Egypt was preparing her invasion, not only did she conduct hostilities by a series of measures that were legal only on the supposition that a state of war existed between herself and Israel, but again and again she sought specifically to justify these measures by insisting that a state of war did in fact exist.

On June 13, 1949, the spokesman of the Egyptian Foreign Ministry said, "We are still in a state of war with the Jews even though the Egyptian Army has ceased to fire."

The Egyptian representative on the UN Special Committee, on June 12, 1951, said, "We are still legally at war with Israel. An armistice does not put an end to a state of war. It does not prohibit a country from exercising certain rights of war." (The "right" in question was that of the blockade.)

The Egyptian foreign minister, Mahmoud Fawzi, said on August 16, 1951, "The Egyptian-Israeli general armistice agreement does not include any provision on the termination of the legal or technical state of war between Egypt and Israel."

And in June 1955, Abdul Nasser said, "Egypt is still technically at war with Israel."

Israel became a state by a recommendation made on August 31, 1947, by the Special Committee for Palestine of the UN. The recommendation was that Palestine should be partitioned into Jewish and Arab states bound by an economic unit. It fell far short of

What Prospects? 181

Jewish aspirations and expectations but when the recommendation was approved by the UN General Assembly on November 29, by 33 votes to 13, with 10 abstentions—more than the necessary two-thirds majority—the Jews accepted. The Arabs refused it outright and warned the General Assembly that they would prevent its implementation with the use of force. They proceeded to do so, and the Jews countered force with their semi-illegal, semi-secret defense force, Haganah, and two terrorist gangs (the Stern Gang and the Irgun), which the Haganah denounced.

By the resolution of the UN, the State of Israel was to come into existence on May 14, 1948. By that date the British were to withdraw from Palestine. They left it in chaos. Violence had spread throughout the country during the previous four months. The Arab Legion, with its British officers, was moved from Jordan, to whom it belonged, into Palestine. But on Israel's birthday, David Ben-Gurion, the first prime minister, appealed to the world, to his Arab neighbors, and to the UN to "assist the Jewish people in the building of its state and to admit Israel into the family of nations."

Ben-Gurion said, "In the midst of wanton aggression, we yet call upon the Arab inhabitants of the State of Israel to preserve the ways of peace and play their part in the development of the state, on the basis of full and equal citizenship and due representation in all its bodies and institutions—provisional and permanent.

"We extend our hand in peace and neighborliness to all the neighboring states and their people, and invite them to cooperate with the independent Jewish nation for the common good of all."

On that same day, at a press conference of the Arab League, its secretary general, Azzam Pasha, replied as follows, "This will be a war of extermination and momentous massacre which will be spoken of like the Mongolian massacres and the Crusades."

Azzam Pasha was referring to the events of that morning, Israel's May birthday, on which she was subjected to simultaneous and coordinated attacks by the organized military forces of five Arab states, members of the Arab League. Lebanon came from the north, Syria from the northeast, Jordan from the east, Iraq moved in through Jordan with the latter's permission, and Egypt advanced from the south.

Some of these armies were formidably armed. All of them had artillery; Egypt and Syria had tanks; Jordan, Iraq, and Egypt had armored cars; Iraq, Egypt, and Syria had, between them, 60 military aircraft. Jordan had the famous Arab Legion, which had been trained and led for a decade by British officers and was armed with British equipment. Against these organized armies Israel had the Haganah, equipped only with small arms, apart from 3 old guns, museum pieces, a few home-made armored cars, no military aircraft, no artillery, no tanks. To the world, there seemed no hope of survival for the new state. It is said that Britain began negotiating with the Italian government for the humane evacuation of the Jewish population from Palestine—her birthday gift to the new state.

At that time, as it does today, the Arab League held the same views as those expressed more recently by King Saud of Saudi Arabia, when he said, "The only way the Arab states must go is to draw Israel up by her roots. Why should we not sacrifice ten million of our fifty million Arabs so that we may live in greatness and honor?"

In four weeks of fighting, all five of the Arab Armies suffered military defeat. On June 11, 1948, a one-month truce was arranged by the Security Council. When it expired, the Arabs refused to prolong it, and on July 9 resumed hostilities. Again they were defeated. Again a truce was called, and again it was broken. On this occasion the Arabs denied Israel certain of the facilities which the truce had allowed her, and it was Israel who attacked. Figting continued throughout the autumn and winter until, between February and July 1949—with Israel's territory much enlarged beyond her birthday boundaries—a series of armistice agreements was concluded between each of the Arab states, with the exception of Iraq. Iraq has always remained, and still remains, technically at war with Israel. The other Arab states have been technically in a state of armistice. The distinction is pedantic.

Each of those armistice agreements had a common preamble: "The Parties . . . responding to the Security Council's Resolution of 16 November 1948 . . . and in order to facilitate the transition from the present truce to permanent peace in Palestine" agreed to four articles: that the injunction of the Security Council should be scrupulously respected; that neither party should take any aggressive action; that each party had the right to freedom from fear; and that the establishment of the armistice was an indispensable step toward the restoration of peace.

To restore peace the General Assembly of the UN appointed a Palestine Conciliation Committee which called a conference at Lausanne in April 1949. By this time there was the problem of the Arab refugees from Palestine, both in Jordan and in the Gaza Strip.

I cannot now discuss at length the whole problem of the refugees, since it would need a book to itself. I will mention only four factors which I think are incontrovertible. First, the Arabs are as much to blame as the Jews for the existence of the refugee problem, and they are more to blame than the Jews for its continuance. There is no doubt that many of the refugees left their homes because they were genuinely afraid of what would happen to them if they remained. On the other hand, the Jews did everything they could to persuade the Arabs to remain in their villages. They issued formal proclamations urging them to do so and guaranteeing their safety; they put up posters and distributed leaflets to the same effect; and local Jewish commanders conferred with local Arab leaders, often on a cordial basis, requesting the Arabs to keep away from the hostilities and to remain in their villages. It was the Arab governments who ordered all Arabs to withdraw from their homes, promising them that "in three weeks' time" they would be back "with their property increased threefold by land, houses, chattels, and women taken from the Jews."

Second, those Arabs who stayed in Israel have been fairly treated. In 1948 the Arab population of Palestine was 700,000.

Of these, only 100,000 remained where they were. They have now increased to 183,000, of which 45,000 are Christians and 20,000 are Druses, and they have their own local councils, their own judges, and their own representatives in the Knesset or Parliament. Although they are excused from National Service, they get all the state benefits such as free education and the health services.

Third, during the seven years that followed the armistice agreements of 1949, the Arab League has adamantly resisted any attempt by the UN to solve the refugee problem. The refugees, particularly those in the Gaza Strip, have been invaluable propaganda to be used against Israel.

Fourth, it was always a physical, political, and economic impossibility to restore the Arab refugees to their former homes. The world is littered nowadays with tragic problems of persons displaced from their countries from one cause or another. (Was it ten or twenty million that were rendered homeless by India and Pakistan between them?) And it has had to be accepted that, in every single case, repatriation was the one solution that could not ever be made to work. Therefore some other solution has always been sougnt.

A solution was strenuously sought oy the Palestine Conciliation Committee at Lausanne in April 1949. Israel was ready to discuss the refugee problem as a part of the general settlement. Her delegation arrived with full authority and with draft proposals for the permanent ending of hostilities, mutual guarantees of friendliness, resort to international arbitration, and the adjustment of boundaries. With regard to the refugees, she offered to pay full compensation and to discuss all aspects.

The Arab delegates, for their part, refused even to meet the israeli delegates, so that the Palestine Conciliation Committee, in the role of brokers, had to conduct separate negotiations between the two parties. This was exactly the same thing that had nappened in Whitehall at the so-called "Round Table Conference" of 1939 when the Arabs, so far from agreeing to sit at the same table with the Jewish delegates, declined even to enter the building by the same doorway. At Lausanne, after weeks of complete frustration, the Palestine Conciliation Committee was unable to take one single step toward converting any of the armistice agreements into that "permanent peace" which was its objective.

During the years that followed, between 1949 and October 1956, Israel had issued frequent pleas for peace. On May 8, 1950, Moshe Sharett, then foreign minister of Israel, wrote to the chairman of the Palestine Conciliation Committee, "I wish to reaffirm categorically that the Government of Israel is willing to negotiate with any state which announces its readiness to conclude a final settlement of all outstanding questions with a view to the establishment of permanent peace. The Government of Israel requires no concessions or undertakings in advance of such negotiations, it being understood that any party having claims to make will be entitled to put them forward in the course of the negotiations . . ."

On November 30 of the same year, Sharett repeated this offer, in fuller terms, to a committee of the UN; and on December 14, still more forcefully to the General Assembly. In 1951, on September 21, the Israel delegation to the Palestine Conciliation Committee, at its Paris conference, repeating once again its "earnest desire to see permanent peace established between Israel and her Arab neighbors, not only for the sake of the Middle East but of the world as a whole," proposed, as a starting point, a series of nonaggression pacts with each of the Arab states. The proposal was ignored by the Arabs.

The offers continued in 1952. On January 9, Mr. Abba Eban, in a statement to a committee of the General Assembly, said, "We have offered to sit with Arab representatives separately or collectively; in the Near East or in Europe, with or without the presence of United Nations representatives; formally or informally to negotiate a peace settlement or a nonaggression pact, or a revision of the armistice agreements. We have offered to discuss the refugee problem in association with, or in separation from, the general context of interstate relations. . . . That offer continues to hold good." It was repeated again before the General Assembly a fortnight later. Again and again, these and similar offers were repeated by Abba Eban at the UN, and by Moshe Sharett and David Ben-Gurion in the Knesset. On May 8, 1954, Nasser told a press conference, "Israel is an artificial state that must disappear."

In November 1955, Mr. Ben-Gurion declared in the Knesset, "I am prepared to meet with the prime minister of Egypt and with every other Arab ruler as soon as possible in order to achieve a mutual settlement, without any prior conditions. The Government of Israel is also ready for a lasting and enduring peace settlement, and for long-term political, economic, and cultural cooperation between Israel and its neighbors. If the other side is not yet ready for that, we would also agree to a limited settlement . . ."

These offers have occasionally inspired an outspoken refusal to negotiate with Israel, but have more often been met by silence. Nasser himself, for instance, has very rarely endorsed personally the full and frank views expressed almost daily on his government-controlled radio and in his government-inspired newspapers. The other Arab rulers have committed only occasional indiscretions. Faris el-Khouri, premier of Syria, when speaking on the subject of American arms aid offered for defense against Russia, said, "We shall take this American arms aid and attack Israel. I take upon myself the responsibility to justify this position before the United Nations. . . . The principal question is that the means of attack shall be at our disposal."

In the Syrian Parliament he declared, "Peace with Israel is inconceivable. Even if the refugees are restored to their country, we shall not on any account make peace with Israel. The Arabs will not agree to peace so long as the Jews remain in the heart of the Arab states. The first round, unfortunately, was unsuccessful. There is no doubt that the Arabs will prepare for the second round and will devote all their energy to its preparations."

In 1954 King Hussein, in his "Speech from the Throne" to the Jordan Parliament, said, "There will be neither peace nor negotiations with Israel."

The official broadcasting stations have been less reticent. On November 16, 1954, Cairo radio declared, "Egypt sees Israel as a cancer endangering the Arab people. Egypt is the physician who can uproot this cancer. . . . Egypt does not forget that it is her obligation to take revenge and she is mobilizing all her forces in anticipation of the hoped-for day." That is only one example of a multitude of similar warnings. On June 13, 1955, the government-controlled Radio Damascus replied to Ben-Gurion's offer of peace: "This desire to hold a meeting with the Arab states is tantamount to the recognition of Israel's existence. This trick is transparent to the Egyptian revolutionary government which rejected the Jewish proposal." The simple answer of the Arab states to Israel's offers of peace has always been that Israel does not exist and so cannot negotiate. And if she does exist, the Arabs intend shortly to destroy her, so that negotiations would be pointless.

This attitude was maintained even at the expense of the Arabs' own recognized interests. There was a project, which later became known as the "Johnston Plan," to divert water from the Jordan and Yarmuk Rivers for the irrigation of large areas of land on which some 150,000 of the refugees could have been settled, and from which much of the Negev could have been made fertile. In 1954 and 1955, Eric Johnston, the special envoy of President Eisenhower, made frequent visits to Israel and the Arab countries to get this scheme approved and put into operation. Israel made concession after concession regarding the proportion of water which she herself would draw from the scheme, until at last it was approved by the technical representatives of all the Arab countries. It was only then that the Arab governments rejected the plan outright, on the grounds that it implied cooperation with Israel and thus, indirectly, the recognition of Israel's existence.

What the Arabs could not accomplish with their five armies they now attempted by economic measures. For years past there had been a balance of trade in the Middle East, Palestine exporting machinery and manufactured goods to her Arab neighbors in exchange for food and raw materials. This trade was now stopped. Israel's next obvious markets were in East Africa and Asia, where she could sell such products as cement, agricultural machinery, and fertilizers, all badly needed by the expanding economies of these countries, in exchange for raw materials. This trade, in turn, was to be almost stopped by the closure of both the Suez Canal and the Gulf of Aqaba to ships trading with or from Israel.

These economic measures were highly effective and, after a few years, began to have a crippling effect on the economy of the new state. General Neguib, in an interview given to *U.S. News and World Report* on March 27, 1953, when asked whether or not he intended to renew active hostilities against Israel, answered, "Why should I endanger my country and lose the confidence of all the big nations? They would consider me aggressive. We are now doing better without war by blockading Israel."

Egypt had established a general blockade against Israel on May 15, 1948, the day after her Army launched its first attacks. The Egyptian Navy had been instructed to search ships passing through the canal with the object of preventing "contraband goods from reaching Israel." This was of course illegal under the Constantinople Convention of 1888. Nor did the blockade cease with the signing of the armistice. In 1950 Egypt issued a list of goods which might not be shipped to Israel under penalty of confiscation, including such articles as chemicals, petroleum, machinery, and motor cars. The blockade became more rigorous until, in 1951, Israel appealed to the Security Council.

At the Security Council Egypt defended her use of the blockade on the grounds (as quoted earlier) that she was still legally at war with Israel and that the operation of the blockade was therefore within her rights. On September 1, 1951, the Security Council rejected the Egyptian argument and called upon her to stop the blockade forthwith. This was one of the few occasions on which Russia did not exercise her veto, but voted with the rest of the Security Council.

While the General Assembly of the UN cannot pass resolutions, but can only make recommendations, the resolutions of the Security Council amount to an international order, which is not only a moral, but also a legal, obligation on all nations. The resolution of September 1, 1951, called upon Egypt ". . . to terminate the restrictions on the passage of international commercial shipping and goods through the Suez Canal wherever bound and to cease all interference with such shipping beyond that essential to the safety of shipping in the Canal itself and to the observance of the international conventions in force." In that same document the Security Council noted that "the restrictions on the passage of goods through the Suez Canal to Israel ports . . . together with sanctions applied by Egypt to certain ships which have visited Israel ports represent unjustified interference with the right of nations to navigate the seas and to trade freely with one another, including the Arab States and Israel."

This resolution of the Security Council was ignored, not only by Egypt, but by all the great powers. None of them did anything to implement it—not even Britain, who, at that time, was in military control of the canal. And Egypt, encouraged by the attitude of the great powers, now extended her blockade still further and began to confiscate goods that could not possibly be classed as "strategic materials" on their way to or from Israel. On October 31, 1952, the Norwegian ship *Rimfrost,* bound from Eritrea to Haifa, was detained at Port Said and its cargo of frozen meat was confiscated. On September 2, 1953, a cargo of motor cars assembled in Israel and consigned to Kenya was confiscated from the Greek freighter *Parnon.* On December 14, 1953, a cargo of meat from Eritrea to Israel was confiscated on board the Italian ship *Franca Mari.* In September 1954, the Israel ship *Bat Galim* was stopped in the Suez Canal; its cargo of meat and hides was seized and its whole crew was imprisoned in Egypt. On July 8, 1955, a consignment of motor bicycles to Israel was taken off the Dutch ship *Fedala.* On July 5, 1956, the Swedish freighter *Birkaland* was stopped on its way to the Far East. One member of her crew, who was found to be holding an Israel passport, was taken off the ship and imprisoned. On October 29, 1956, a few hours before the Sinai operations started, the Dutch ship *Fedala* was stopped for a second time, and her cargo—this time of meat—was confiscated.

Apart from ships which were actually trading with Israel, or which had happened to call at Haifa on their way from anywhere in the world to somewhere else, Egypt prepared a "black list" of ships which had ever, at any time, carried goods either to or from Israel. This comprised over 70 ships, of which 43 were British, 13 Scandinavian, 8 United States, 6 Dutch, and 2 Russian. Any vessel whose name appeared on this black list had to undergo a rigorous search, was denied all services such as bunkering, water, and repairs, and was subjected to long delays in transit through the canal. Its crew was not allowed ashore in any Egyptian port.

Meanwhile, Egypt had extended her measures to the Gulf of Aqaba, as was described in Chapter II. Ras Nasrani and Sharm el Sheikh were evacuated of their inhabitants, Arab fishermen, in favor of substantial military garrisons and naval batteries. Very large sums were spent on their fortification, and the gulf was closed.

Egypt issued a decree concerning the Gulf of Aqaba and this has been renewed annually on July 15 each year. It defined the "prohibited area" as a circle with a radius of 20 nautical miles, its center being at Sharm el Sheikh and its eastern boundary the coast of Saudi Arabia. All nations were formally warned that any aircraft crossing this boundary would be shot at, and that any aircraft contravening the regulations would be held on their first landing at any Egyptian airport. If the aircraft belonged to a scheduled airline which was operating with the authorization of the Egyptian government, such authorization would be "liable to withdrawal" and no further permits to fly over Egyptian territory would be issued to any aircraft belonging to that airline.

Although Egypt gave an assurance that innocent passage into, and out of, the Gulf of Aqaba would be permitted, the American ship *Albion* and the British ship *Anshun* were both fired on. These ships were in fact trading not with Israel, but with Jordan. The *Anshun* had been chartered to carry Muslim pilgrims to Mecca.

All traffic to or from the Israeli port of Elath at the head of the gulf was completely stopped.

It is now a matter of simple addition to discover that the ships of no less than nine countries, all members of the UN, including the United States, had been subjected to illegal measures which the Security Council had specifically condemned in 1951.

These economic measures were not confined to the blockade. Three years before Israel became a state, the Arab League had established a policy of boycott, and a central office in Damascus, with branches in every major Arab city, to put it into effect. Its declared object was to sabotage the industrialization of Palestine by Jews and to obstruct the export of "Zionist goods." It was not very easy, in those days, to decide what were Zionist goods and what were not; but once Israel had become a state, the problem was simpler.

After 1949 the boycott was extended to all nations doing business of any sort with Israel, and the technique of the black list was extended from shipping to industry. No industrial firm or company which sold goods to Israel, or which bought her produce, would be permitted to trade with any Arab state. To implement their boycott the Arab states used their diplomatic missions. In 1952, they tried to interrupt the Bonn government's reparations agreement with Israel, whereby dispossessed Jews were paid compensation in manufactured goods from Western Germany. But the Bonn government resisted and the reparations continued to be paid.

Israel's oil supplied from Arab sources had of course been cut off, and she was now dependent on oil from Mexico. The Arab League warned Mexico to discontinue deliveries. Mexico refused to do so.

The boycott became not only anti-Israeli but anti-Jewish. Industrial firms in America, Great Britain, Holland, and elsewhere, when tendering for contracts, were often required to fill in a questionnaire stating the number of Jewish employees, Jewish directors, and the degree of Jewish management. If they declined to answer, their tenders were, in theory, rejected. It did not always work. A British firm, Medo-Chemicals Ltd., was told that it would get no clearance certificate for medical supplies required by a hospital in Iraq unless it established that there were no Jews on its board of directors. But when it refused to comply, the clearance certificate was granted.

As I have already mentioned, most of the international agreements governing air traffic had been abrogated by the Arab League. No aircraft which was bound to or from Israel might fly over Arab territory. Saudi Arabia declared that it would shoot down any aircraft flying over its territory which had previously landed in Israel. And no aircraft that had called at Lydda on its route could land at the airport of any Arab state. Israel made no corresponding boycott; her airports were open to all civilian aircraft, not excluding those from Arab states.

The Arab League now suspended those international agreements which existed for the safety of civil aircraft. No communication between ground and air, such as meteorological warnings or flight directions, no matter what the emergency, was permitted to aircraft of any line which had called at Lydda Airport. The issue of flight information from Lydda itself was jammed and the safety of all air traffic in the area thereby imperiled. On April 9, 1954, an Air France plane, on its way from Rome to Lydda, had engine trouble over Beirut and was losing altitude. Beirut Airport refused permission to land or even to give information. It was only by luck that the plane was able to reach Israel territory. On January 3, 1954, a British Skyways aircraft, en route from Lydda to Teheran, had engine trouble and was forced to make an emergency landing at Baghdad. Three Israeli passengers were arrested and imprisoned by the Iraqi authorities for four months.

Israel did not reciprocate these measures. An aircraft belonging to Air India was forced by bad weather to land at Lydda Airport on its way to Cairo. Aboard the plane there was an Egyptian diplomat. He was not allowed to leave the airport but, until the flight could continue, was imprisoned in the transit restaurant. There he was fed at Israel's expense and given books to read printed in

Arabic and English. When interviewed by Israeli correspondents, he said that he had been "splendidly well treated." But after the aircraft was able to continue its flight, taking him to Cairo, he was wise enough to describe to the Egyptian press his "brutal reception in Jewish-occupied Palestine."

The Arab League next extended its boycott into the corporate body of the UN and its specialized agencies, as already noted.

The Arab attitude in this respect is governed by a decision of the Arab League, taken in February 1951, when it was agreed: that no representative of Israel should be allowed into any Arab country to attend any international conferences; that no Arab country would send delegates to any international conference in any non-Arab country if Israel had also been invited; and that no Israeli employees of any international organization would be allowed to enter any Arab country in the course of his official duties.

The various "specialized agencies" of the UN could do little to defend the rights of their members—or even of their own officials if they happened to be Jews. When UNESCO sent a circular to all countries asking what facilities would be given to educational experts, both Jordan and Lebanon replied to the effect that no Jews, no matter what their nationalities, would be allowed to enter their countries, even if they were officials of UNESCO.

In August 1955, there was an FAO conference on locusts held in Damascus for all member countries of the Middle East. It was attended also by many representatives from European countries, and even from Russia. Israel was excluded. This was a matter of particular importance to Israel, since war could be waged against locusts only by operations extending over a wide area. Moreover, Israel could have made a considerable contribution to the common good, since her scientists have made great progress in this field. Again, when WHO organized conferences to deal with such diseases as malaria, dysentery, tuberculosis, and bilharzia—all of which are very prevalent in the Middle East, but have been almost eradicated in Israel (with the exception of course of tuberculosis)

—Israel was again excluded from either making a contribution by her scientists or benefiting from the experience of others.

Recently some of these specialized agencies have developed a new technique for dealing with this situation. When UNESCO organized a conference on vocational training in rural areas, it was agreed that the Egyptian government should send out the invitations but that the expenses should be met from UNESCO finances, to which Israel contributes. Egypt insisted that Israel should not be invited to the conference, so that Israel found herself financing her own boycott by Egypt. In a recent UN report on technical assistance, Israel was excluded altogether, so that the Arab states would not be offended by finding themselves mentioned with Israel in the same document.

Meanwhile the armistice agreements had not brought physical peace to Israel's frontiers. Between 1949 and 1955, there were 2494 clashes with armed infiltrators from Arab countries, and 280 acts of sabotage in Israel. During this period 360 men, women, and children were killed and 733 wounded. All of these incidents preceded the start, in 1955, of the fedayeen activities.

The word "fedayeen" means "self-sacrifice." This form of self-sacrifice was honored by a huge papier-mâché statue which was set up in Suleiman Pasha Street in the middle of Cairo for the annual parade which celebrates the "anniversary of the liberation." It represents the fedayeen: a uniformed gunman who stands four stories high, between whose mammoth legs the traffic flows and the military procession passes. He is a brave monument to the hundreds of men, women, and children killed or wounded, scores of burnt houses, blown wells, mined roads, and civilian traffic ambushed, all during the last two years. There have been five attacks on railways, which might be called military objectives—although the railways are rarely used in Israel for military purposes—but apart from these, there has not been a single case of fedayeen attack on a military target.

The reward for fedayeen activities was regular pay, augmented

What Prospects?   195

by a cash commission for each proven atrocity. From documents taken in Gaza it is now known that the sort of proof offered by the fedayeen included trophies such as an ear or finger cut from a corpse, a child's blood-stained copybook, or a family photograph spattered with blood.

The fedayeen were not only paid, but also trained, by the Regular Egyptian Army. Their special technique soon became familiar and could be distinguished from that of other marauders or criminals coming from across the borders. Soon this technique was detected in raids launched from Syria and Jordan, as well as from the Gaza Strip. It was then suspected—and later confirmed by prisoners under interrogation—that Egypt was sending her fedayeen into Syria and Jordan to operate from across their frontiers. There is no doubt that this was done with the knowledge and connivance of the Syrian and Jordanian governments since, in November 1955, various bases for fedayeen activities by Egyptian personnel were established in those countries—for instance, at Jenin, Nablus, Hebron, and the police stations (later destroyed in "reprisal raids" by Israel) at Gharandal, Rahwa, and Kalkilya. Some of these bases were actually in charge of Egyptian officers. Elsewhere they were supervised by the Egyptian military attaché.

In between raids—it is now known—many of the fedayeen were contriving, unknown to UNRWA officials, to live on UNRWA rations issued in the refugee camps of Gaza. This was contrary to regulations, since those who were earning wages were not permitted, technically, to be nourished at the expense of the UN.

From the beginning of 1955 onward, some form of fedayeen raids took place on almost every night. There was virtually no means of defense open to Israel. More than half of her population comprises Oriental Jews, many of whom are very recent immigrants; and some 180,000 Arabs are Israeli citizens. The fedayeen, who could not be distinguished in the dark from Oriental Jews or Israeli Arabs, could cross the frontier almost anywhere they liked. It would take a million men to guard Israel's frontiers against this kind of infiltration, and the total population of Israel is 1,750,000.

Nevertheless, it is the foremost duty of government to secure the physical defense of its citizens. The only method of doing so available to Israel was either to respond in kind, or to take military measures by way of reprisals or deterrents. Unwilling to take the former course, Israel adopted the latter. After a certain number of incidents in any particular district, she responded with an organized military attack, usually in the same area, but invariably against military targets.

Speaking of these operations, General Dayan said, "Indirectly the reprisals serve as a demonstration of the Israel–Arab balance of power as it will appear to the Arab governments. . . . Also it means that Israel considers the infiltration as an intolerable act of hostility and instructs her forces to cross the border and strike at the Arab countries. She does not consider it an act of vengeance. It is a punitive action and a warning that if the country concerned does not control its inhabitants and prevent their striking at Israel, the Israeli forces will wreak destruction in their country."

For two reasons the world generally failed to realize what was happening. In the first place, the pattern of events invited distortion in the world's newspapers. There might be a dozen fedayeen incidents, in each of which a few civilians were killed. Each might be worth an obscure paragraph of newsprint. They would be followed by a large-scale reprisal, on the part of Israel, which was usually worth a column and sometimes a banner headline. Hence the impression was spread that, even if Israel was not the aggressor, she was as much to blame as her neighbors.

In the second place Israel, as I have said earlier, has virtually no public-relations services—apart from a few odd departments here and there operating in a manner which is unbelievably amateurish. Despite my boundless respect for Mr. Ben-Gurion, and my deep admiration for General Dayan both as a soldier and as a person, I consider it disastrous that these two men cannot acknowledge the need to use modern methods of informing the world about what is happening in Israel and what are her true aspirations. I doubt if any country has ever been more gravely misunderstood—and it is

What Prospects? 197

her own fault. The world was not even made aware that, for instance, the reprisal raids at Gharandal, Rahwa, and Kalkilya were directed exclusively against fedayeen headquarters known as such to Israel's intelligence service.

Nor does the world realize how, again and again, Israel has attempted to find some solution, other than the reprisal raid, that would ensure frontier peace. On June 6, 1955, she suggested to the secretary general of the UN that direct high-level talks should be held between Egypt and herself. Egypt rejected these proposals on June 13 on the grounds that to hold such talks would be "tantamount to recognizing Israel's existence."

After protracted efforts by Major General Burns—chief of staff of the UN Truce Supervision Organization (UNTSO)—Egypt at last agreed to open negotiations, but only on the question of the Gaza border, and only within the framework of the Mixed Armistice Commissions (MAC). The first meeting took place on June 28, 1955. After twelve further meetings, lasting until August 24, during which the fedayeen activities continued, Egypt walked out of the negotiations.

A new outbreak of fedayeen activities followed, and there were seven separate attacks during the night of August 27, in which ten civilians were killed and a number wounded. While lodging a protest with the UN, Israel attacked a fedayeen barracks at Khan Yunis in the Gaza Strip, where the fedayeen had their central headquarters, and demolished it completely.

Until this time Egypt had denied any knowledge of the fedayeen activities and had attributed them to the individual acts of refugees in Gaza. But on August 26, the day before Khan Yunis was blown up, Radio Cairo officially announced for the first time that "an Egyptian patrol had entered Israeli territory for the purpose of chasing an Israeli patrol"; and on August 31, Cairo spoke on her radio directly to Israel: "The Egyptian fedayeen reached but a few kilometers from your capital. . . . They killed and blasted and put to an end every hope of that Zionism that brought you into being. What hope remains for you, O Israel? Egypt has decided to send you her heroes, the grandchildren of Pharaoh and the sons of the Arabs and Islam. And they shall purify the soil of Palestine. Thus prepare yourselves, shed your tears, wail and moan, for the day of your extermination draws near. . . . There will be no peace on your borders because we demand revenge—and revenge means the death of Israel."

Throughout the remainder of 1955, and for the first three months of 1956, the cycle of fedayeen raids and Israeli reprisals continued on the same pattern. Usually, after a large-scale reprisal, there would be peace for a while on that particular sector. Then, in April 1956, fedayeen activity increased sharply. In five days there were 64 attacks in which 14 people were killed. These included 14 ambushes on the highway, 9 separate raids on border settlements, and 22 acts of sabotage, mainly against wells, water pumps, and cisterns.

At the end of April, Mr. Dag Hammarskjold negotiated a new cease-fire which was immediately violated by Egypt. Cairo Radio announced on May 15: "The war is not now confined to firing or attacks along the border, but has reached the heart of Israel and places which were believed to be safe from danger. . . . The quiet reigning in the villages and towns remote from armistice lines has turned to terror."

Nasser paid a visit to fedayeen units at their headquarters in Khan Yunis and told them, "You have proved by your deeds that you are heroes upon whom our entire country can depend. The spirit with which you entered the land of our enemy must spread." On April 12, fedayeen had entered a children's school, whose pupils were mostly orphans from Nazi-occupied Europe, and had opened fire on them while they were at prayer. Three were killed, 3 more died on the way to hospital, and 7 others were wounded.

During June and July the frontiers were quieter. Then came the Suez crisis, and fedayeen activities were almost completely suspended during the period of international discussions when Anglo-French operations seemed imminent. When the likelihood of such intervention diminished, the fedayeen resumed their operations in September and October.

On September 10 they blew up a part of the Beersheba railway, and on September 11 Israel responded by blowing up Rahwa police station, a fedayeen base. On September 12, three Druse watchmen were killed at Ein Ofarin, and Israel responded by blowing up another fedayeen base in the police station at Gharandal. On September 23, when a conference of archaeologists at Ramat Rahel was fired on from a Jordan military emplacement some 600 yards distant, there were 21 casualties of which 3 were killed. And during the next few nights there were further incidents in which a woman was murdered while picking olives and a tractor driver was killed while plowing near the Jordan border. Israel replied by blowing up the police station at Husan.

On Octooer 4 two civilian cars were ambushed on the S'dom–Beersheba road, close to the Jordan frontier, and five people were killed. Five days later two workmen were killed at Even Yehuda and their ears were cut off—doubtless to support a claim for a bonus. There were a number of other frontier incidents in this district, the fedayeen coming from Kalkilya, a well-known fedayeen base in a Jordanian village close to the frontier. The base was in the police station, and this was the target against which Israel delivered a large-scale reprisal. Her troops captured the area, evacuated the building, and then demolished it.

The operation, like its predecessors, was conducted with strict orders that on no account were any civilians to be injured. Compliance with this order meant that Israeli troops had to spend a period of hours on the objective, in the course of which they suffered some 23 casualties, which could have been avoided only at the risk of killing or injuring Jordanian civilians. In fact, the fedayeen base was very neatly extracted. Not even the neighboring houses were structurally damaged, and no civilian was hurt. But the cost was prohibitive. If such casualties were to be accepted, it would be better to stage an operation on a still larger scale which, it was hoped, would put an end to the fedayeen once and for all, and establish peace on the frontiers. Hence the Sinai Campaign—which cost Israel 174 killed and 4 taken prisoner.

So much for the past. What of the future? The situation (at the time of writing) is still farcical. Israel was invaded, at the moment of her birth, by the armies of five Arab states. She beat the lot of them. Ever since, she has been trying to make peace with them. They have refused even to negotiate; they have declared that they are still at war with Israel; they have continued to make war by all means short of a second invasion by their regular armies. This invasion was being prepared. Israel struck first and again won a decisive victory. This was the only possible means of making her enemies negotiate. She wants nothing else; she has no territorial ambitions; she is not asking for peace on her own terms; all she wants is peace negotiations. These have been denied her by the action of the UN and the United States in support of Nasser.

Nasser had justified his illegal blockade, and his murder of civilians by fedayeen, on the grounds that he was at war with Israel. He had no grounds for complaint when Israel made war in return. Nor had he any status with the UN when he appealed to it. He had ruled himself out of court by his repeated rejection of all the efforts of the UN to restore peace and specifically by his refusal to obey the Security Council resolution of September 1, 1951.

Why did the UN intervene to save Nasser the dictator, the international criminal, the man who had persistently disobeyed the UN? Why did the United States do so? The uncharitable say that it was because of her oil interests in the Middle East. The charitable say that it was because she was bluffed and panicked by Russia into believing that the Third World War was about to start. Be that as it may, at the time of writing the United States is still supporting Nasser while Nasser *still* says that he is at war with Israel; and the United States is still putting economic pressure on Israel to make sure that she gives up all the physical security that she has gained by her campaign and all her chances of negotiating peace.

What Prospects? 201

At the time of writing, the United States (through the UN) is still demanding that Israel evacuate *unconditionally* both the Gaza Strip and Sharm el Sheikh. The Gaza Strip was never a part of Egypt until she took it by her own unprovoked aggression in 1948, since when she has used it as a base for fedayeen warfare against Israel's civilian population. She won it by force of arms and she has now lost it by force of arms. She has no possible claim to reoccupy it, and Israel would be mad to give it back again to a dictator who declares himself to be still at war with her.

As for Sharm el Sheikh, Egypt threw out its few inhabitants and spent millions of pounds on its fortification for no purpose except to close the Gulf of Aqaba to Israel's shipping. In doing so she affirmed that she was exercising a blockade which was legal because she was still at war with Israel. Israel would be mad to evacuate Sharm el Sheikh except on the conditions that Egypt will never refortify it and never resume her blockade in the Gulf of Aqaba.

The United States, by insisting that Israel evacuate unconditionally the Gaza Strip and Sharm el Sheikh, is sowing the seeds of another war, watering those seeds, and giving them a lavish dose of fertilizer. If Egypt resumes fedayeen activities from the Gaza Strip, and if she resumes the blockade of Israel's shipping—indulging in both activities on the basis that she is at war with Israel— Israel will have no alternative but to give her another bloody nose and another kick in the pants. Surely this cannot be what the United States wants?

To make sure that I am not suspected of being anti-American, I must indulge in a few sentences of personal vanity. During World War II, I spent much of my time serving with United States forces; I landed with United States assault troops at both Casablanca and Sicily; on occasion I have worn the American uniform with pride; I served with General Patton in North Africa; I was twice given medals by President Roosevelt in reward for my services under General Eisenhower. I doubt if there is any non-American who has a greater affection for America than myself. It is from this affection that I view the farce and the tragedy of the United States attitude. And it is from this affection that I venture to suggest the concrete steps that the United States can take to bring about peace.

Israel's objective is peace in the full and positive sense of that word: friendship with her Arab neighbors, reciprocal trade, full and free international communications; and she is prepared to go to considerable lengths, and to make concessions, to get them. At the same time, she realizes that this is a long-term ideal, and that it must be reached step by step. The first step is to start negotiations. Since the Arabs will not recognize Israel's existence, they cannot negotiate. Therefore they must be made to do so by the UN—which means, in effect, by the United States.

If once the Arabs and the Israelis can be brought to sit at the same table, there is very great hope that progress toward peace will result. But the system of brokerage by the UN will not work. It was tried by Britain at the so-called Round Table Conference of 1939; it was tried by the Palestine Conciliation Committee of the UN at Lausanne ten years later. In each case, when the Arabs declined to enter the same room as the Jews, the conciliators got nowhere at all by the hopeless procedure of negotiating with each party separately. It is not a system that can ever be fruitful in any issue where Arabs are involved. It is not compatible with the way in which the Arab mind works.

On the other hand, direct bargaining is very likely to be effective. Once the Arabs can be induced to begin bargaining, their whole mentality changes. Bargaining is a fundamental activity in the Middle East; it is a recognized procedure; it is almost a ritual. If an Arab starts to bargain, he intends to make a deal and he reckons himself a failure if he cannot conclude one. Remember, the blood feud is still a very live factor amongst most Arabs; but a blood feud which has existed for forty years can be settled in forty minutes—and is often so settled—provided the procedure is correct.

What Prospects? 203

Once the Arabs start negotiating or bargaining, they are bound to recognize that they have a great deal to gain from peaceful coexistence, and indeed cooperation, with Israel. Reciprocal trade would be enormously to the advantage of the Arab states, and Israel could make important technical contributions to their economic and social prosperity. But until the actual process of bargaining begins, such factors do not even exist in the Arabs' calculations.

What agency can induce or, if necessary, compel the Arabs to start negotiations? During the last seven years, the UN has shown that it can do nothing in the Middle East until the United States pushes it into action. In the past, the powers that imposed peaceful solutions in the Middle East were Britain and France. These two powers have now been rendered impotent, so far as the Middle East is concerned, by the action of the United States during the Suez crisis. Therefore the responsibility of imposing peace on the Middle East which, I must repeat, means first imposing negotiations, rests upon the United States. What can the United States do about it?

It is not an easy question to answer. Russia wants trouble in the Middle East; Israel is a godsend to Russia; Russia needs troubled waters in this area, because fishing in troubled waters is her own specialty, her particular way of waging modern war against the West. Accordingly, the United States is not anxious to force Egypt into negotiating peace with Israel, because of the fear that if undue pressure is brought to bear on Nasser, he will turn still more fully to Russia and will depend, even more than hitherto, on Russian assistance.

I believe that this fear is groundless. Short of starting a Third World War, Russia cannot do a great deal more in the Middle East than she has already done. And if Russia intends to start a Third World War, she will not choose the Middle East in which to do so. Strategically speaking, it is the most awkward theater of war for Russian operations.

In any event, there is one step which the United States, through the UN, can take immediately without any fear of active Russian intervention—because such intervention would not be practicable. This is the demilitarization of Sinai. This would obviously be for the good of everyone and everything, except Nasser and his dictatorial ambitions. If Sinai is demilitarized, Israel cannot attack Egypt, and Egypt cannot attack Israel.

How is this to be done? The obvious method of taking a step which is so clearly in the interests of world peace would be by a resolution of the Security Council. But Russia would probably veto any such resolution. Therefore the step must be taken by way of a recommendation of the General Assembly of the UN. And the obvious nature of the step would be the occupation of the Sinai Peninsula by an international force until such time as Egypt agrees to negotiate a peace treaty with Israel, and until that treaty is signed. But the present international force is in Egypt only with Egypt's permission. Egypt has to be told that the international force will not be withdrawn, nor will she be allowed to reoccupy Sinai, until she has made peace.

I wonder if the United States is yet persuaded that peace in the Middle East is essential to world peace? In the context of this speculation, it is worth recalling the events of November 8, 1956, when Israel agreed to withdraw her Army from Sinai. The pressure that was then brought upon her was fantastic. Eisenhower wrote a personal letter; so did Hammarskjold; Bulganin sent a brutal note. Israel knew—and I think the world now knows—that Bulganin's note was bluff. But President Eisenhower did not. Eisenhower acted, inadvertently of course, as Bulganin's agent. Unable to see that Russia's bluff was intended mainly, and perhaps only, to distract attention from Hungary, he threw the whole weight of the United States behind Egypt.

On the evening of November 8, Mr. Herbert Hoover, Jr., United States under-secretary of state, sent a personal message by Israel's ambassador in Washington to Mr. Ben-Gurion, saying, "If you do not withdraw your troops from Sinai, you personally will be responsible for the outbreak of the Third World War." No responsible prime minister of a small nation, and certainly no person of Ben-Gurion's caliber, could withstand a message such as this.

By that message, President Eisenhower recognized that war in the Middle East was likely to mean the start of the Third World War. He now has to accept the complementary proposition that peace in the Middle East is essential to world peace, and that peace in the Middle East has to begin with peace between Israel and Egypt. Once Egypt agrees to negotiate peace, all the other Arab nations will do the same. And if President Eisenhower were to exert on Nasser the same pressure that he exerted on Ben-Gurion, all the other Moslem countries in the world, except Syria and possibly Jordan, would reinforce it.

Personally I believe that, if the United States is prepared to exercise the responsibility which she has assumed by her intervention, and if she would compel Egypt to enter into peace negotiations, then Israel ought to take certain measures to improve the prospects of such negotiations in advance. She has already missed a great chance of forcing the world to recognize the simplicity and the truth of her aspirations. When she first captured the Gaza Strip, she could surely have issued some bold and imaginative proposals, in general terms, for the solution of the refugee problem. She could have said that she would take perhaps 20,000 of them back within her own frontiers; that another 50,000 could have been settled in the area between Gaza and El Arish, where there are sources of water, which, in the Middle East, means prosperity; and that another 50,000 could have been settled in parts of Sinai where water could be brought from the Jordan and the Yarkon Rivers.

There would have remained then some 90,000 refugees to be settled elsewhere. They could be taken easily by their fellow Arabs to the latter's advantage. Many of the Arab countries are grossly under-populated; they have large areas of potentially fertile land which are entirely undeveloped; their national economies would benefit greatly by the settlement in these areas of Arab refugees, provided funds were available for their establishment. Such funds already exist, earmarked for that very purpose, in the coffers of the UN. Iraq alone could take at least 100,000 refugees and would benefit economically from doing so. Even if Israel did miss the chance of making some such bold and imaginative offer at the psychological moment, she still has the chance of declaring to the world the kind of terms on which she is anxious to negotiate peace with her Arab neighbors. I believe she is afraid of doing so because in the past such offers have always been entirely fruitless. Indeed they have reacted to her disadvantage. Whenever she has proposed to make a concession, provided the Arabs did the same, it has always been assumed thereafter that this concession could be required of her, even if the Arabs made none in response. In particular, this was her experience with the armistice agreements of 1949.

Those agreements failed because the UN, who sponsored them, had no Great Power behind it. The United States has now put itself behind the UN. Israel ought to be able to assume that, with the United States supporting the UN in the seat of justice, a just settlement could be reached. On this assumption she could risk suggesting a basis for negotiations in the first place. But the United States has not so far given Israel any grounds for overcoming her rational reluctance and taking any such risk.

The first step toward peace in the Middle East has to be taken by the United States. Nobody else can do it. The negotiations for peace have to be started. And this leaves only one more thing to be said. I must repeat it yet again so that the right word is the last word of this book: Israel went to war only in order to secure peace; Israel wants only peace.

Milton Keynes UK
Ingram Content Group UK Ltd.
UKHW020958090124
435730UK00015B/455